Patricia Grace was born in Wellington, New Zealand, in 1937. She is of Ngati Raukawa, Ngati Toa and Te Ati Awa descent, and is affiliated to Ngati Porou by marriage. Her collection of stories, *Waiariki*, the first published collection by a Maori woman, came out in 1975. She has written children's books, of which *The Kuia and the Spider* won the 1982 New Zealand Children's Picture Book of the year; and novels, including *Potiki* (The Women's Press, 1987), winner of the fiction section of New Zealand Book Awards in 1987, and the Liberaturpreis in Germany in 1994; *Mutuwhenua: The Moon Sleeps* (Livewire Books for Teenagers, The Women's Press, 1988); and *Cousins* (The Women's Press, 1993).

Patricia Grace has taught in primary and secondary schools and was the Writing Fellow at Victoria University in Wellington in 1985. She is married with seven children.

D0032269

Also by Patricia Grace from The Women's Press:

Potiki (1987)
Mutuwhenua: The Moon Sleeps (Livewire Books for
Teenagers, 1988)
Cousins (1993)

the *sky people*

Patricia Grace

Published in Great Britain by The Women's Press Ltd, 1995
A member of the Namara Group
34 Great Sutton Street, London EC1V oDX

First published in New Zealand by Penguin Books (NZ) Ltd, 1994

Copyright © Patricia Grace 1994

The right of Patricia Grace to be identified as the author of
this work has been asserted by her in accordance with the
Copyright, Designs and Patents Act 1988.

British Library Cataloguing-in-Publication Data
A catalogue record for this book is available from the British
Library

This book is sold subject to the condition that it shall not, by
way of trade or otherwise, be lent, re-sold, hired out, or otherwise circulated without the Publisher's prior consent in any
form of binding or cover other than that in which it is published and without a similar condition including this condition
being imposed on the subsequent purchaser.

ISBN 0 7043 4415 7

Printed and bound in Great Britain by BPC Paperbacks Limited,
Aylesbury, Bucks

For
Irihapeti Ramsden and Ron Te Kawa

And in memory of
Metapere McGill and Harata Solomon

'Who are the Sky People? The Haurangi, the
Wairangi, the Porangi—those crazy from the wind or
what they breathe, those crazy from the water or what
they drink, those crazy from darkness or depression. I
know someone who is all three.'

(In conversation with Keri Kaa)

My thanks to the Literature Committee of Queen Elizabeth II Arts Council for assistance while writing *The Sky People*.

My special thanks to He Ara Hou Maori Theatre, who work with the spirit birds. The idea for 'Sweet Trees' has come directly from their work.

Contents

Contents

Sun's Marbles

When Maui booby-trapped Sun then clobbered him over the head with a hunk of bone shaped like two parts of a bootmaker's last, he won, for all time, high praise as the pioneer of daylight saving.

It was a surprise attack.

It was a violent act.

During the beating, which was resolute and prolonged, Sun lost some of his marbles, most of which went skittering out to stardom. Some, however, dropped to Earth, who caught them tidily, although she didn't really want them because she understood that these pretty things could be dangerous. But she was stuck with them. She couldn't send them back because Gravity was so lopsided, so she hid them deep in her pockets.

Earth had an instinct for hiding things. In the early days when she and Sky were close together, hiddenness had been a way of life. Everything had been hidden between these two. Light could not penetrate and there was no room to swing a cat's ancestor.

There was no 'above' and 'below' in those days. No direction was different from any other — no 'vertical', 'horizontal' or 'diagonal' as Earth and Sky rolled together in each other's arms. Or alternatively, every position was above or below, every direction was north, south, east and west, every angle was vertical, horizontal or diagonal. But there was no superiority and Challenge had not been born, even though there was an inkling of it in the minds of some of Earth and Sky's children. There was the potential.

Parents speak to each other in double language, spell out secrets so that children will not understand what they are talking about. But children get an inkling, if not of the content of the secret, then at least of the idea that there is a secret, something to be discovered, to be gleaned from whisperings if they keep on listening in the dark, keep adding one little piece of nothingness to another.

Earth and Sky were born out of Darkness and therefore knew about Light, and this was the secret they wanted to keep to themselves so that their children would remain children, keep their innocence and stay with them forever.

But the children were patient listeners, and blind, innocent and squashed between their ever-embracing parents as they were, they got to talking. The listeners and decoders of secret language among them had worked out that there was something else. There was something being kept from them by their parents and they would not be satisfied until they found out what it was. It was to do with otherness, other realms, the other side. It was when the children first talked to each other about these matters that Dissatisfaction was first expressed, but not clearly expressed and not clearly understood.

What came out of the discussion was that there was a desire by most of the children to have greater understanding. If they were to have greater understanding, then their known world had to be changed.

They had to get outside of it somehow, but they were bound on all sides by the locked bodies of their parents. They were squashed and breathless and realised they would have to separate their parents if they were to become free. How were they to do this from their position of powerlessness?

There were Plants, but none of them were upright and were only as vines creeping about in the dark. There was Water, but it was stagnated and lifeless. There was Wind, but it was only as stale breath. Conflict, being a metaphor for People, was only the beginnings of an idea.

So the offspring of Sky and Earth began trying to move the parents away from each other, pushing, pulling, prising, but were not successful until Plant Life stopped creeping about, tried standing, then just kept on doing what it normally did — that is, grow — but from a different perspective. That's when Perspective and Direction began to be understood. After some eras Sky was lifted off Earth by upwardly mobile Plant Life and the children found out about Light.

Wind had been the dissenter from all this, and after the big event became angry with all those who had had anything to do with separating his mother and father. So he called up northerlies, southerlies, easterlies, westerlies, nor'westers, sou'-easters, storms, hurricanes and tornadoes — and stirred up chaos amongst Plants and Waters and the Creatures who, now that there was Light and Space, had been released among them.

It was while Wind was having his tantrums that Earth realised that some of her kids needed protection against others, and she did her best to hide some of the less protected ones until it was safe for them to come out again. She had fought long and hard against being separated from Sky, but now that it was done she was determined to make the best of the situation.

Well, all this Light. All this Space. It was almost too much of a good thing. Plants and Creatures spread everywhere. Water became seas, lakes and rivers, and became inhabited by Swimmers. Eventually People made an appearance, but this didn't happen without a great deal of trauma, which included incest, personality change, family break-up and solo parenthood.

In spite of all this Earth and Sky did the best they could to be good providers. They tried to take an interest in what was happening.

When the latest addition came along, these People, Earth

and Sky were fascinated and pleased and thought that living apart and allowing Light and Space had some compensations after all. In fact they indulged these latest offspring, gave them free rein, but soon found that the more they were given the more they wanted.

These Johnny-come-latelies reckoned life would be better if they had a bit more daytime, even though they were told they should be grateful for what they had. In the olden days their ancestors had had no daylight at all. This kind of talk fell on deaf ears.

Anyhow, Maui was the one who took up the cause on People's behalf. Maui was a foundling, who in his formative years hadn't known his true parentage; and he was born ugly, which didn't help matters. But to offset these seeming disadvantages he was of impeccable stock and had a mother who saw opportunities and was prepared to give him up at birth in order that his gifts be allowed to develop. Also he was part human — a combination of Worldly and Other Worldly — so it was appropriate that he should be the one to act as a go-between for People.

In taking up the challenge to lengthen daylight he beat up Sun so badly that Sun hobbled about like an old koroua and from then on took many hours to travel across the face of Sky.

And that was when Earth, seeing the beating handed out to Sun, hid Sun's marbles away because she knew instinctively that they would be dangerous in the wrong hands. She knew that these latest, very demanding offspring were not mature enough to take responsibility for them.

Later on, this same Maui, who must have learned Irresponsibility from the human side of his genealogy, went to get Fire for his earthly cousins. Because of the immature way he handled the situation, Fire had to be sent to hide in the bodies of trees so that Maui and these earthlings wouldn't play fast and loose with it.

Anyway, these Teina, younger sisters and brothers of Winds, Waters, Plants, Animals, Birds, Insects, Reptiles and Fish, were really too big for their boots. Upstarts. In many ways they took after Maui, being Potiki, last born. Like Maui they had outsized attitude problems and didn't care what happened or who got hurt as long as they got their own way.

These ones had no idea of how to look after their own best interests either, and without the approval of those more mature and knowledgeable than themselves, began to change the order of things.

They began to kill their Tuakana — that is, their older brothers and sisters — without good reason, and to destroy their living places. The more powerful ones among them stole food and took over the living places of the less powerful ones of their own tribe too.

And they weren't satisfied with that. They'd heard about Sun's marbles and that Earth had hidden them somewhere. They knew they'd never be happy until they found them, and they began to search. They made great holes all over Earth, shifting or destroying Plants and Animals as well as the powerless members of their own tribe.

At last they found Sun's marbles in Earth's deepest pockets and with these they made objects in their own likeness — that is, they made objects capable of enormous destruction that were not able to be properly controlled. During the making of these objects there was so much waste that many of their own tribe had to be shifted away from their homes to make room for it, many had to run in fear of it. Many had nowhere to go and had to live with it. They became ill and maimed, gave birth to sick children, died painfully.

Sun could do nothing on the day when he rose, unaware, and was straightjacketed by Maui's snare. And when that bone came cracking down on him, chipping off bits, he could only hold tight and hope his days weren't ended.

Sky is no butterfingers and was deft in gathering in Sun's marbles, and though it was no accident that he allowed a few to go Earthward, he later came to regret this.

It was instinct that caused Earth to tuck these bright things away. Neither she nor Sky realised at the time that their children could become their enemies, or that they themselves could be enslaved. They were indulgent parents inclined to put unacceptable behaviour down to teething problems, hyperactivity, high intelligence or precocity.

But later they began to ask themselves where they'd gone wrong. Was it because of their separation that these children had become so grasping, so out of control? Had Sky been too distant? Had Earth been too over-compensating? What could they have done about it anyway? Was it all a question of Light?

Flower Girls

When the big man died people began arriving at the gates at five in the morning, waiting to be called at daylight, shifting in their coats and rugs and passing the envelope. Cigarette tips spotted the dark.

While one group was being called, more cars and buses would arrive and another group would prepare itself. This kept up throughout two days from early morning to nightfall.

The women doing the calling and the men making the speeches had to have a rotating system so they could have time to eat and sleep. The cooks never got off their feet, nor did those who were cleaning and setting up tables every hour, and nor did the ones who were bringing in supplies.

Once it became obvious that the usual facilities wouldn't cope with the numbers of people arriving, a marquee was put up as an extra dining room and truckloads of mattresses were borrowed from another marae and put down in the assembly hall of the local college.

Both out on the marae and in the house many words were spoken about the man and his work. The family itself, as well as the managers of catering, accommodation and protocol, made sure that nothing that could be done was left undone in order to honour the man at the time of his attaining his ultimate chieftainship. Visitors came with full envelopes to put down.

The big man wasn't big. He was small in build and stature, and the brothers and nephews who carried him into the meeting house held a light load.

When the lid was removed, and beneath the flow of words from the minister and as the cloaks, ornaments, photographs and flowers were placed, there was satisfaction expressed that a good job had been done by the undertakers. This husband, father, brother, cousin, friend, who had become a bone of his usual self during his illness, now appeared as if in reasonable health. In fact he was young and smooth again, round-cheeked almost. His jaw had been tightened into a suggestion of a smile to show that he had died peacefully.

His sister and sister-in-law were the ones who had seen to it that he was dressed in his best for his final journey and that his badges, service medals and ribbons were displayed in a suitable way amongst the more ancient treasures on the casket.

So everything was all right. Everything was as it should have been for such a man — that is, except for the blight of his daughters all named after flowers. They were Hyacinth, Violet, Lilac, Verbena and Marigold.

Hyacinth was the most unflowerlike. Summer and winter, over her great pod of a body, she wore sleeveless tent dresses splitting beneath pouchy underarms. Curved under her bluish rolls of feet she wore jandals no matter what the weather. Her face was a great round cake. In fact she had two faces, the large cake-face being centred by the little face that had been hers when she was a girl. She was butter-coloured, untouchable, and she wheezed in late on that first day smelling of mutton and cabbage, crying hideously for Daddy.

No one would have thought it inappropriate for Hyacinth to cry and call out for her father if she'd been anywhere in sight during the time of his illness. But he'd been in hospital, dying, for some weeks before being brought home to spend the final week of his life. In all that time she'd visited him just once. That one time she'd been up and down, in and out like a fretting animal. So calling for Daddy now, splashing tears, keeping the minister waiting, didn't go down very well with those who knew.

And afterwards, instead of staying there by the man, Hyacinth left the meeting house and went to the dining room, where she bungled about getting in the way of workers who were trying their best to respect her as a bereaved daughter. Two aunts came out and cornered her at last, spoke hard in her ears and took her out to the house, where they put a rug round her shoulders and sat her by her mother. The sister and sister-in-law managed to keep her there, shut up, for the rest of the day.

Violet came in at dusk on the first day wearing a full-length leather coat with fur collar and lapels, dosed to the eyeballs and unable to manage her own two feet. She had left home at fifteen to tote herself up and down the waterfront. It was an easy way to make money, though it wasn't money she wanted then. If she had been asked what it was she wanted, she may not have been able to bring to articulation the word 'forgetting'. But it was 'forgetting' that being laid, paid, robbed and jabbed with cigarette ends could help her do.

At nineteen she married a man of moderate means, and in the five years after that had three children.

But she had a habit as well. In the end she left the children with their father and went back to business. In spite of all this, deep inside herself she knew she was half sensible. She could feel it sometimes. One day she'd beat the habit, find Roxy, Maadi and Palace, who would love and adore her, and there'd be a new life for all of them.

When this Violet came in, strung between two friends, it was some younger cousins who managed to put the coat and her belongings into the boot of a car for safekeeping, roll her in a blanket and put her into a corner amongst the pillows, out of the way, faintly snoring.

Lilac was the one who had been saved by the Lord, but it was only her soul that had been saved. Sickness was eating away at all the guilty places of her, and the women had made a bed up for her by the man and helped her to get comfortable there. Medication allowed her to sleep, and each time she woke, the aunts washed her face and hands, tidied her hair and propped her up on pillows.

The one called Verbena had become unhinged years before, and during the time of her father's illness had had to be re-admitted to hospital while the family coped. No one could stop her from laughing. She wasn't brought in until the evening of the second day, tranquillised but still giggling. However, people knew they should tolerate this. Verbena was a loved one, a special one, as was Lilac too. This was mentioned several times in speeches so that everyone would understand.

Marigold, who was the youngest, had run away to save her-self when she was ten. She'd been encouraged to do this by Lilac, the good one, and had spent two years living on the streets, sleeping under bridges and in old buildings. She'd learned to steal and sniff glue, but somehow she felt this wasn't really her style. One day she went looking for Violet, of leather and fur, who took her in, gave her clothes and thirty dollars and told her to go and get a room, a job as a waitress and to work herself on from there, which she did.

Her first job was in an all-night café, midnight until eight in the morning, and what she liked most about it was being warm in the night and eating. At the time of her father's death she was working as a receptionist-cashier in a restaurant specialising in deep-fried family meals. Sometimes for this job she was required to wear clown clothes, pirate outfits or animal suits, and to paint her face up in different ways. This was something she enjoyed. She was beige-coloured and had eyes like sea anemones. She had a boyfriend too, and a taste for top shelf.

Now she was twenty and, though she came home fortified with bourbon, she was, at least, on her own two feet, which were in their own diamante stockings and in their own spike-heeled shoes. She was the last of the sisters to arrive. Because she had left home at such an early age, she knew nothing of protocol and strode onto the marae in her skimp of a skirt and sat at the end of the paepae, chewing. But she was put into place after a while, with only the next day to go.

All of these flower-named ones had been beautiful and sister-looking when they were little girls, was what everyone said. The aunts were nearly exhausted as they went about doing what they could to make the behaviour of the sisters less conspicuous.

It was the mother, wife of the man, that everyone felt sorry for. She deserved better in the way of daughters, especially at a time like this. She'd been a true support to the man in all that he did. She'd been a loving mother. It was said over and over again.

Actually the aunts could've wished for a little more responsiveness from their sister at this time. The occasional trickle from their sister's eyes they thought insufficient, really, though when they thought about it they realised she'd always been pasty. And they didn't think the smock and cardigan appropriate either for such a big occasion, but they were kind and didn't say so. After all, their sister was exhausted after their brother's long illness and there was not one daughter with sense enough to be of use to her.

However, on the day of the burial they insisted on lending her some clothes. They couldn't let the newly widowed sister send their brother off dressed the way she was, not when he'd always been so particular. It was bad enough the daughters being circuses.

They helped her while she dressed, and locked themselves either side of her when the time came to follow the casket to the cemetery ahead of the large crowd.

At the graveside the mother just waited the time through, letting go a thin sigh as the shovels mounded the last of the earth over the big man. After that she allowed herself to be taken back to the wharenui, and allowed herself to be cheerful when it was the right time.

She was the only one who knew what good girls her daughters really were. They were good girls, deserving of the names of flowers, who had kept the secret of themselves and the big man — kept the secret, kept the secret, kept the secret.

Ngati Kangaru

Billy was laughing his head off reading the history of the New Zealand Company, har, har, har, har.

It was since he'd been made redundant from Mitre 10 that he'd been doing all this reading. Billy and Makere had four children, one who had recently qualified as a lawyer but was out of work, one in her final year at university, and two at secondary school. These kids ate like elephants. Makere's job as a checkout operator for New World didn't bring in much money and she thought Billy should be out looking for another job instead of sitting on his backside all day reading and laughing.

The book belonged to Rena, whose full given names were Erena Meretiana. She wanted the book back so she could work on her assignment. Billy had a grip on it.

Har, har, these Wakefields were real crooks. That's what delighted Billy. He admired them, and at the beginning of his reading had been distracted for some minutes while he reflected on that first one, E. G. Wakefield, sitting in the clink studying up on colonisation. Then by the time of his release, EG had the edge on all those lords, barons, MPs, lawyers and so forth. Knew more about colonisation than they did, haaar.

However, Billy wasn't too impressed with the reason for EG's incarceration. Abducting an heiress? Jeepers! Billy preferred more normal, more cunning crookery, something funnier — like lying, cheating and stealing.

So in that regard he wasn't disappointed as he read on, blobbed out in front of the two-bar heater that was expensive to run, Makere reminded him. Yes, initial disappointment left him the more he progressed in his reading. Out-and-out crooks, liars, cheats and thieves, these Wakefields. He felt inspired.

What he tried to explain to Makere was that he wasn't just spending his time idly while he sat there reading. He was learning a few things from EG, WW, Jerningham, Arthur and Co., that would eventually be of benefit to him as well as to the whole family. He knew it in his bones.

'Listen to this,' he'd say, as Makere walked in the door on feet that during the course of the day had grown and puffed out over the tops of her shoes. And he'd attempt to interest her with excerpts from what he'd read. ' "The Wakefields' plan was based on the assumption that vast areas — if possible, every acre — of New Zealand would be bought for a trifle, the real payment to the people of the land being their 'civilising' . . ." Hee hee, that's crafty. They called it "high and holy work".

'And here. There was this "exceptional Law" written about in one of EG's anonymous publications, where chiefs sold a heap of land for a few bob and received a section "in the midst of emigrants" in return. But har, har, the chiefs weren't allowed to live on this land until they had "learned to estimate its value". Goodby-ee, don't cry-ee. It was held in reserve waiting for the old fellas to be brainy enough to know what to do with it.

'Then there was this "adopt-a-chief scheme", a bit like the "dial-a-kaumatua" scheme that they have today where you bend some old bloke's ear for an hour or two, let him say a few wise words and get him to do the old rubber-stamp trick, hee, hee. Put him up in a flash hotel and give him a ride in an aeroplane then you've consulted with every iwi throughout Aotearoa, havintcha? Well, "adopt-a-chief" was a bit the same except the prizes were different. They gave out coats of arms, lessons in manners and how to mind your p's and q's, that sort of stuff. I like it. You could do anything as long as you had a "worthy cause",' and Billy would become pensive. 'A worthy cause. Orl yew need is a werthy caws.'

On the same day that Billy finished reading the book he found his worthy cause. He had switched on television to watch *Te Karere*, when the face of his first cousin Hiko, who lived in Poi Hakena, Australia, came on to the screen.

The first shots showed Hiko speaking to a large rally of Maori people in Sydney who had formed a group called Te Hokinga ki Aotearoa. This group was in the initial stages of planning for a mass return of Maori to their homeland.

In the interview that followed, Hiko explained that there was disillusionment among Maori people with life in Australia and that they now wanted to return to New Zealand. Even the young people who had been born in Australia, who may never have seen Aotearoa, were showing an interest in their ancestral home. The group included three or four millionaires, along with others who had made it big in Oz, as well as those on the bones of their arses — or that's how Billy translated into English what Hiko had said in Maori, to Hana and Gavin. These two were Hana Angeline and Gavin Rutene, the secondary schoolers, who had left their homework to come and gog at their uncle on television.

Hiko went on to describe what planning would be involved in the first stage of The Return, because this transfer of one hundred families was a first stage only. The ultimate plan was to return all Maori people living in Australia to Aotearoa, iwi by iwi. But the groups didn't want to come home to nothing, was what Hiko was careful to explain. They intended all groups to be well housed and financed on their return, and discussions and decisions on how to make it all happen were in progress. Billy's ears prickled when Hiko began to speak of the need for land, homes, employment and business ventures. '"Possess yourselves of the soil,"' he muttered, '"and you are secure."'

Ten minutes later he was on the phone to Hiko.

By the time the others returned — Makere from work, Tu from
job-hunting and Rena from varsity — Billy and the two children
had formed a company, composed a rap, cleared a performance
space in front of the dead fireplace, put their caps on backwards
and practised up to performance standard:

First you go and form a Co.
Make up lies and advertise
Buy for a trifle the land you want
For Jew's harps, nightcaps
Mirrors and beads

Sign here sign there
So we can steal
And bring home cuzzies
To their 'Parent Isle'

Draw up allotments on a map
No need to buy just occupy
Rename the places you now own
And don't let titles get you down
For blankets, fish hooks, axes and guns
Umbrellas, sealing wax, pots and clothes

Sign here, sign there
So we can steal
And bring home cuzzies
To their 'Parent Isle'

Bought for a trifle sold for a bomb
Homes for your rellies
And dollars in the bank
Bought for a trifle sold for a bomb
Homes for your rellies and
Dollars in the bank

Ksss Aue, Aue,
Hi.

Billy, Hana and Gavin bowed to Makere, Tu and Rena. 'You are looking at a new company,' Billy said. 'which from henceforward (his vocabulary had taken on some curiosities since he had begun reading histories) will be known as Te Kamupene o Te Hokinga Mai.'

'Tell Te Kamupene o Te Hokinga Mai to cough up for the mortgage,' said Makere, disappearing offstage with her shoes in her hand.

'So all we need,' said Billy to Makere, later in the evening, is a vast area of land "as far as the eye can see".'

'Is that all?' said Makere.

'Of "delightful climate" and "rich soil" that is "well watered and coastal". Of course it'll need houses on it too, the best sort of houses, luxury style.'

'Like at Claire Vista,' said Makere. Billy jumped out of his chair and his eyes jumped out, 'Brilliant, Ma, brilliant.' He planted a kiss on her unimpressed cheek and went scrabbling in a drawer for pen and paper so that he could write to Hiko:

' . . . the obvious place for the first settlement of Ngati Kangaru, it being "commodious and attractive". But more importantly, as you know, Claire Vista is the old stamping ground of our iwi that was confiscated at the end of last century, and is now a luxury holiday resort. Couldn't be apter. We must time the arrival of our people for late autumn when the holidaymakers have all left. I'll take a trip up there on Saturday and get a few snaps, which I'll send. Then I'll draw up a plan and we can do our purchases. Between us we should be able to see everyone home and housed by June next year. Timing your arrival will be vital. I suggest you book flights well in advance so that you all arrive at once. We will charter buses to take you to your destination and when you arrive we will hold the official welcome-home ceremony and see you all settled into your new homes.'

The next weekend he packed the company photographer with her camera and the company secretary with his notebook and biro, into the car. He, the company manager, got in behind the wheel and they set out for Claire Vista.

At the top of the last rise, before going down into Claire Vista, Billy stopped the car. While he was filling the radiator, he told Hana to take a few shots. And to Gavin he said, 'Have a good look, son, and write down what the eye can see.'

'On either side of where we're stopped,' wrote Gavin, 'there's hills and natral vejetation. There's this long road down on to this flat land that's all covered in houses and parks. There's this long, straight beach on the left side and the other side has lots of small beaches. There's this airport for lite planes and a red windsock showing hardly any wind. One little plane is just taking off. There's these boats coming and going on the water as far as the I can see, and there's these two islands, one like a sitting dog and one like a duck.'

Their next stop was at the Claire Vista Information Centre, where they picked up street maps and brochures, after which they did a systematic tour of the streets, stopping every now and again to take photographs and notes.

'So what do I do?' asked Tu, who had just been made legal adviser of the company. He was Tuakana Petera and this was his first employment.

'Get parchments ready for signing,' said Billy.

'Do you mean deeds of title?'

'That's it,' said Billy. Then to Rena, the company's new researcher, he said, 'Delve into the histories and see what you can come up with for new brochures. Start by interviewing Nanny.'

'I've got exams in two weeks I'll have you know.'

'After that will do.'

The next day Billy wrote to Hiko to say that deeds of title were being prepared and requested that each of the families send two thousand dollars for working capital. He told him that a further two thousand dollars would be required on settlement. 'For four thousand bucks you'll all get a posh house with boat, by the sea, where there are recreation parks, and amenities, anchorage and launching ramps, and a town, with good shopping, only twenty minutes away. Also it's a good place to set up businesses for those who don't want to fish all the time.

'Once the deeds of sale have been made up for each property I'll get the signatures on them and then they'll be ready. I'll also prepare a map of the places, each place to be numbered, and when all the first payments have been made you can hold a lottery where subscribers' tickets are put into "tin boxes". Then you can have ceremonies where the names and numbers will be drawn out by a "beautiful boy". This is a method that has been used very successfully in the past, according to my information.

'Tomorrow we're going out to buy Jew's harps, muskets, blankets (or such like) as exchange for those who sign the parchments.'

'You'll have a hundred families all living in one house, I suppose,' said Makere, 'because that's all you'll get with four thousand dollars a family.'

'Possess yourselves of the homes,' said Billy.

'What's that supposed to mean?'

'It's a "wasteland". They're waste homes. They're all unoccupied. Why have houses unoccupied when there are people wanting to occupy them?'

'Bullshit. Hana and Gav didn't say the houses were unoccupied.'

'That's because it's summertime. End of March everyone's gone and there are good homes going to waste. "Reclaiming and cultivating a moral wilderness", that's what we're doing, "serving to the highest degree", that's what we're on about, "according to a deliberate and methodical plan".'

'Doesn't mean you can just walk in and take over.'

'Not unless we get all the locks changed.'

By the end of summer the money was coming in and Billy had all the deeds of sale printed, ready for signing. Makere thought he was loopy thinking that all these rich wallahs would sign their holiday homes away.

'Not *them*,' Billy said. 'You don't get *them* to sign. You get other people. That's how it was done before. Give out pressies — tobacco, biscuits, pipes, that sort of thing, so that they, whoever they are, will mark the parchments.'

Makere was starting to get the hang of it, but she huffed all the same.

'Now I'm going out to get us a van,' Billy said. 'Then we'll buy the trifles. After that, tomorrow and the next day, we'll go and round up some derros to do the signing.'

It took a week to get the signatures, and during that time Billy and the kids handed out — to park benchers in ten different parts of the city — one hundred bottles of whisky, one hundred packets of hot pies and one hundred old overcoats.

'What do you want our signatures for?' they asked.

'Deeds of sale for a hundred properties up in Claire Vista,' Billy said.

'The only Claire Vistas we've got is where our bums hit the benches.'

'Well, look here.' Billy showed them the maps with the allotments marked out on them and they were interested and pleased. 'Waste homes,' Billy explained. 'All these fellas have got plenty of other houses all over the place, but they're simple people who know nothing about how to fully utilise their properties and they can "scarcely cultivate the earth". But who knows they might have a "peculiar aptitude for being improved". It's "high and holy work", this.'

'Too right. Go for it,' the geezers said. Billy and the kids did their rap for them and moved on, pleased with progress.

In fact everything went so well that there was nothing much left to do after that. When he wrote to Hiko, Billy recommended that settlement of Claire Vista be speeded up. 'We could start working on places for the next hundred families now and have all preparations done in two months. I think we should make an overall target of one hundred families catered for every two months over the next ten months. That means in March we get our first hundred families home, then another lot in May, July, September, November. By November we'll have five hundred Ngati Kangaru families, i.e., about four thousand people, settled before the holiday season. We'll bring in a few extra families from here (including ourselves) and that means that every property in Claire Vista will have new owners. If the Te Karere news crew comes over there again,' he wrote, 'make sure to tell them not to give our news to any other language. Hey, Bro, let's just tap the sides of our noses with a little tip of finger. Keep it all nod nod, wink wink, for a while.'

On the fifth of November there was a big welcome-home ceremony, with speeches and food and fireworks at the Claire Vista hall, which had been renamed Te Whare Ngahau o Ngati Kangaru. At the same time Claire Vista was given back its former name of Ikanui and discussions took place regarding the renaming of streets, parks, boulevards, avenues, courts, dells and glens after its reclaimers.

By the time the former occupants began arriving in mid-

December, all the signs in the old Claire Vista had been changed and the new families were established in their new homes. It was a lovely, soft and green life at that time of the year. One in which you could stand barefooted on grass or sand in your shorts and shirt and roll your eyes round. You could slide your boat down the ramp, cruise about, toss the anchor over and put your feet up, fish, pull your hat down. Whatever.

On the day that the first of the holidaymakers arrived at 6 Ara Hakena, with their bags of holiday outfits, Christmas presents, CDs, six-packs, cartons of groceries, snorkels, lilos and things, the man and woman and two sub-teenagers were met by Mere and Jim Hakena, their three children, Jim's parents and a quickly gathering crowd of neighbours.

At first, Ruby and Gregory in their cotton co-ordinates, and Alister with his school friend in their stonewash jeans, apricot and applegreen tees, and noses zinked pink and orange, thought they could've come to the wrong house, especially since its address seemed to have changed and the neighbours were different.

But how could it be the wrong house? It was the same windowy place in stained weatherboard, designed to suit its tree environment and its rocky outlook. There was the new skylit extension and glazed brick barbecue. Peach tree with a few green ones. In the drive in front of the underhouse garage they could see the spanking blue boat with *Sea Urchin* in cursive along its prow. The only difference was that the boat was hitched to a green Landcruiser instead of to a red Range Rover.

'That's our boat,' said Ruby.

'I doubt it,' said Mere and Ken together, folding their arms in unison.

'He paid good money for that,' a similarly folded-armed neighbour said. 'It wasn't much but it was good.'

Ruby and Alister didn't spend too much more time arguing.

They went back to Auckland to put the matter in the pink hands of their lawyer.

It was two days later that the next holidaymakers arrived, this time at 13 Tiritiroa. After a long discussion out on the front lawn, Mai and Poto with their Dobermen and a contingent of neighbours felt a little sorry for their visitors in their singlets, baggies and jandals, and invited them in.

'You can still have your holiday, why not?' said Mai. 'There's the little flat at the back and we could let you have the dinghy. It's no trouble.'

The visitors were quick to decline the offer. They went away and came back two hours later with a policeman, who felt the heat but did the best he could, peering at the papers that Mai and Poto had produced, saying little. 'Perhaps you should come along with me and lay a formal complaint,' he suggested to the holidayers. Mai, Poto and a few of the neighbours went fishing after they'd gone.

From then on the holidaymakers kept arriving and everyone had to be alert, moving themselves from one front lawn to the next, sometimes having to break into groups so that their eye-balling skills, their skills in creative comment, could be shared around.

It was Christmas by the time the news of what was happening reached the media. The obscure local paper did a tame, muddled article on it, which was eclipsed firstly by a full page on what the mayor and councillors of the nearby town wanted for Christmas, and then by another, derived from one of the national papers, revealing New Year resolutions of fifty television personalities. After that there was the usual nation-wide closedown of everything for over a month, at the end of which time no one wanted to report holiday items any more.

So it wasn't until the new residents began to be sued that there was any news. Even then the story only trickled.

It gathered some impetus, however, when the business-people from the nearby town heard what was happening and felt concerned. Here was this new population at Claire Vista, or whatchyoum'callit now, who were *permanent residents* and who were *big spenders*, and here were these fly-by-night jerk holiday-makers trying to kick them out.

Well, ever since this new lot had arrived business had boomed. The town was flourishing. The old supermarket, now that there was beginning to be competition, had taken up larger premises, lowered its prices, extended its lines and was providing trollies, music and coffee for customers. The car sale yards had been smartened up and the office décor had become so tasteful that the salespeople had had to clean themselves up and mind their language. McDonald's had bought what was now thought of as a prime business site, where they were planning to build the biggest McDonald's in the Southern Hemisphere. A couple of empty storerooms, as well as every place that could be uncovered to show old brick, had been converted into better-than-average eating places. The town's dowdy motel, not wanting to be outdone by the several new places of accommodation being built along the main road, had become pink and upmarket, and had a new board out front offering television, video, heating swimming pool, spa, waterbeds, room service, restaurant, conference and seminar facilities.

Home appliance retailers were extending their showrooms and increasing their advertising. Home building and real estate was on an upward surge as more businesspeople began to enter town and as those already there began to want bigger, better, more suitable residences. In place of dusty, paintless shops and shoppes, there now appeared a variety of boutiques, studios, consortiums, centres, lands and worlds. When the Clip Joint opened up across the road from Lulu's Hairdressers, Lulu had her place done out in green and white and it became Upper Kut.

After that hair salons grew all over town, having names such as Head Office, Headlands, Beyond the Fringe, Hairport, Hair-waves, Hedlines, Siz's, Curl Up and Dye.

So the town was growing in size, wealth and reputation. Booming. Many of the new businesspeople were from the new Ikanui, the place of abundant fish. These newcomers had brought their upmarket Aussie ideas to eating establishments, accommodation, shops, cinema, pre-loved cars, newspaper publishing, transport, imports, exports, distribution. Good on them. The businesspeople drew up a petition supporting the new residents and their fine activities, and this petition was eventually signed by everyone within a twenty-kilometre radius. This had media impact.

But that wasn't all that was going on.

Billy had found other areas suitable for purchase and settlement, and Rena had done her research into the history of these areas so that they knew which of the Ngati Kangaru had ancestral ties to those places. There were six areas in the North Island and six in the South. 'Think of what it does to the voting power,' said Hiko, who was on the rise in local politics. Easy street, since all he needed was numbers.

Makere, who had lost her reluctance and become whole-hearted, had taken Hiko's place in the company as liaison manager. This meant that she became the runner between Ozland and Aotearoa, conducting rallies, recruiting families, co-ordinating departures and arrivals. She enjoyed the work.

One day when Makere was filling in time in downtown Auckland before going to the airport, she noticed how much of the central city had closed up, gone to sleep.

'What it needs is people,' she said to the rest of the family when she arrived home.

They were lounging, steaming themselves, showering, hairdressing, plucking eyebrows, in their enormous bathroom. She let herself down into the jacuzzi.

'Five hundred families to liven up the central city again. Signatures on papers, and then we turn those unwanted, wasteland wilderness of warehouses and office spaces into town houses, penthouses and apartments.' She lay back and closed her eyes. She could see the crowds once again seething in Queen Street renamed Ara Makere, buying, selling, eating, drinking, talking, laughing, yelling, singing, going to shows. But not only in Queen Street. Not only in Auckland. Oh, it truly was high and holy work. This Kamupene o te Hokinga Mai was 'a great and unwonted blessing'. Mind-blowing. She sat up.

'And businesses. So we'll have to line up all our architects, designers, builders, plumbers, electricians, consultants, programmers,' she said.

' "Soap boilers, tinkers and a maker of dolls' eyes" ', said Billy.

'The ones already here as well the ones still in Oz,' Makere said. 'Set them to work and use some of this damn money getting those places done up. Open up a whole lot of shops, restaurants, agencies . . . ' She lay back again with her feet elevated. They swam in the spinning water like macabre fish.

'It's brilliant, Ma,' Billy said, stripping off and walking across the floor with his toes turned up and his insteps arched — in fact, allowing only part of each heel and the ball joints of his big toes to touch the cold tile floor. With the stress of getting across the room on no more than heel and bone, his jaw, shoulders, elbows and knees became locked and he had a clench in each hand as well as in the bulge of his stomach.

'Those plumbers that you're talking about can come and run a few hot pipes under the floor here. Whoever built this place should've thought of that. But of course they were all summer people, so how would they know?' He lowered himself into the water, unlocking and letting out a slow, growling breath.

'We'll need different bits of paper for downtown business properties,' said Tu from the steam bench.

'Central Auckland was originally Ngati Whatua I suppose,' said Rena, who lost concentration on what she was doing for a moment and plucked out a complete eyebrow. 'I'll check it through then arrange a hui with them.'

'Think of it, we can influx any time of the year,' said Billy. 'We can work on getting people into the city in our off-season. January . . . And it's not only Auckland, it's every city.'

'And as well as the business places there are so many houses in the cities empty at that time of the year too,' said Makere, narrowing her eyes while Billy's eyes widened. 'So we can look at those leaving to go on holiday as well as those leaving holiday places after the season is over. We can keep on influxing from Oz of course, but there are plenty of locals without good housing. We can round them all up — the solos, the UBs, pensioners, low-income earners, street kids, derros.'

'Different papers again for suburban homes,' said Tu.

'Candidates and more candidates, votes and more votes,' said Hiko, who had come from next door wearing a towel and carrying a briefcase. 'And why stop at Oz? We've got Maori communities in Utah, in London, all over the place.'

'When do we go out snooping, Dad?' asked Hana and Gavin, who had been blow-waving each other's hair.

'Fact finding, fact finding,' said Billy. 'We might need three or four teams, I'll round up a few for training.'

'I need a video camera,' said Hana.

'Video for Hana,' said Billy.

'Motorbike,' said Gavin.

'Motorbike,' said Billy.

'Motorbike,' said Hana.

'Two motorbikes,' said Billy.

'Bigger offices, more staff,' said Tu and Rena.

'See to it,' said Billy.

'Settlements within the cities,' said Makere, who was still with solos, UB, check-out operators and such. 'Around churches. Churches, sitting there idle — wastelands, wildernesses of churches.'

'And "really of no value",' said Billy. 'Until they become . . .'

'Meeting houses,' Makere said. 'Wharenui.'

'Great. Redo the fronts, change the décor and we have all these new wharenui, one every block or so. Take over surrounding properties for kohanga, kura kaupapa, kaumatua housing, health and rehab centres, radio stations, TV channels . . .'

'Deeds of sale for church properties,' said Tu.

'More party candidates as well,' Hiko said. 'We'll need everything in place before the new coalition government comes in . . .'

'And by then we'll have "friends in high places".'

'Have our person at the top, our little surprise . . .'

'Who will be advised that it is better to reach a final and satisfactory conclusion than . . .'

'". . . to reopen questions of strict right, or carry on an unprofitable controversy".'

'Then there's golf clubs,' said Makere.

'I'll find out how many people per week, per acre use golf courses,' said Rena. 'We'll find wasteland and wilderness there for sure.'

'And find out how the land was acquired and how it can be reacquired,' said Billy.

'Remember all the land given for schools? A lot of those schools have closed now.'

'Land given for the war effort and not returned.'

'Find out who gave what and how it will be returned.'

'Railways.'

'Find out how much is owed to us from sale of railways.'

'Cemeteries.'

'Find out what we've saved the taxpayer by providing and maintaining our own cemeteries, burying our own dead. Make up claims.'

'And there are some going concerns that need new ownership too, or rather where old ownership needs re-establishing . . .'

'Sport and recreation parks . . .'

'Lake and river retreats . . .'

'Mountain resorts . . .'

Billy hoisted himself. 'Twenty or thirty teams and no time to waste.' He splatted across the tiles. 'Because "if from *delay* you allow others to do it before you — they will succeed and you will fail",' and he let out a rattle and a shuffle of a laugh that sounded like someone sweeping up smashings of glass with a noisy broom.

'Get moving,' he said.

House of the Fish

I remember the house of the fish. One night I watched it burn, but it still stands as long as there's someone to remember.

The fish was on the door — the head, bones and vertebrae, where Hopper nailed them after we'd sucked them. Pearl.

It was a door of no colour on a hut of no colour. Or beach-coloured, bleached. In the end there was colour, ruby and amber against an amethyst sky.

There was a yard of packed dirt and chicken droppings mushed, and a salted tree with an axe driven in, branches hung with knives, tin cups, a billycan. Beside the door, roof high, was a criss-cross tangle of wood we'd carried.

Sometimes in perfect windlessness and stillness the old tree would groan, the bones of wood would chatter, the fish would scratch at the door and I would wonder who it was who was passing. I'd call goodbye, tell them not to stop because there was no one here ready to travel their road. 'Go on and make a good journey,' I'd call.

There was a baked track twisting away from the door among stones and spiky bushes where we met lizards on their way to talk to the fish about how they had all once lived together as a tribe. At the end of the track there were severe rocks and looping waters where we found places for our lines to go down, or where we collected the leached wood bones for the fire. Hopper and I.

This was after the land and the people went; after Hopper locked his arms round my leg, shut his eyes and no one could move him.

'We'll come back for both of you soon,' they said. 'You'll have to come soon because they're mowing the houses down.'

They did come back when all the houses were falling. By then I'd worked my way in to the hard place, away from the line of machines, taking with me boards I'd pulled from the old house before it came down. I sat Hopper against the tree while I put our new place together. When our family came they looked all round, looked at Hopper barnacled to my thigh and said, 'We'll come back and get you before the start of winter. You'll have to come then, before the cold sets in.'

'Bring blankets,' I said. 'Bring me a hen.'

They didn't forget. They brought blankets, six hens and a rooster. 'Till he's five,' they said. 'Or before the machines come this way.'

Whenever we came home late with our catch, dragging our branches through the dark, we'd look up when we came to the last bend in the track and see the bone of the fish bringing us home, reeling us in as though it spoke. Against the wall, beside its hollowed eye, and higher than its eye, we'd stack the white wood. We'd hang the knives and the lines in the tree, step out of the salted clothing, light the fire and put the catch in the pan. Then we'd eat by only firelight, unless the moon came in to sit with us. While we ate, or while we lay waiting for sleep to come, I'd tell Hopper the things I know.

I told him about his mother who drowned of sorrow, about how it was Whai the stingray who helped her, felt sorry for her, took her in, perhaps wanted her for his own. Who knows that she could yet be clutched to his underbelly, the two of them riding together the expanses of the worlds?

I had seen Whai at about that time, pale wingtips sliding in and out of the water, one side and then the other, the breadth between wingtip and wingtip so great as to be imponderable.

An evil one lived there once, where Whai now makes his

home. This evil one had the form of a glowing eel that lured people with colours so intense as to be irresistible. At that time Whai was called the Homeless One. Whai and Eel fought for days and nights, and in the end Eel died with Whai's barb through his obsidian heart. During the final lashings of Eel, with the water all round a swirling rainbow, the barb became dislodged and flew out of the sea to the land where it became Peka the perching gull. It happened in the long ago.

Whai has guarded the deep place ever since, making it his home. He will not call people there and will slide his wings out of the water in warning if anyone comes near. But there are those who, despite the warning, will go beyond the point of no return and Whai cannot turn them away.

Hopper's mother was the youngest of our three daughters. She was dark-skinned and green-eyed and her hair was black and fine. She was a happy girl who we dressed in red skirts and who we fed on karengo, corn pudding, fish eyes and tender mouth parts of fish. She was seventeen when the war began and during that time she fell in love.

The war brought the Americans into our valley with rolls of barbed wire which they stretched across the bay. We were manpowered to help dig a large tank trap at the top of the valley, as well as trenches and ditches which, when finished, were mined for the invasion. We were drilled in what to do, where to go, when the enemy landed and when the tanks came riding through. I had visions of the valley blowing in sheets of copper fire, of people scorched and harlequin hurtling towards a flashing sky. But the invasion didn't happen, or not in that way.

I would think of Whai, striding the bay, turning his eye, watching the tall rocks shatter from gunfire when the target practices began.

Tia fell in love with American William Harper and he with her. He loved her truly, I'm convinced of that. He was no deserter and would've returned for her if he'd lived.

The war ended, the bombs and wire were taken away, though the trenches and traps remained. Tia was left with Hopper. She named him William Harper but he soon became Hopper, or Little Amaorican.

During that winter, after Hopper was born, when I noticed that nothing would reflect in our daughter's eyes, I tried to touch and quicken the spirit with stories, the things I knew.

I sat with her during the day and night hours of feeding Hopper, bathing, dressing, tucking down. I talked to her, to them both, attempting to distract her from sorrow so that her spirit could unfold, find its height again, find its light. Now and again I would see it and I'd sing to it, chanting it up all night, sometimes all night and all day long.

At those times her eyes, sometimes her step, would liven and she'd walk out brightly on the tracks or eat a soup of rock oysters that I'd prepared, or hold a little thing — a leaf, a shell and look at it, seeing it in her hand. For a moment here, a moment there, for longer and longer moments she'd be revived. But only some of the time.

That's why I know that it wasn't with intention that she went to Whai's door. I know she went there from carelessness through sorrow, through the spirit not yet reaching its true height, finding its true light.

Also the carelessness was mine. I was the one who knew those things, who knew that anyone must be full-spirited when going to the sea. But I was so pleased that morning when her two older sisters, their husbands and children, called to us on the way to the water and Tia called them to wait for her. I was pleased because I know how the sea can heal.

But I should have gone with her, made sure that she kept to the edges, that she walked only the shore rocks, stayed in the waves of shore. Stronger places are for those who are well and full. I could have put Hopper across my shoulders in a blanket and gone with them. But I was happy to let her go while Hopper slept.

I watched them going. There was a clear view in those days, over the stones, the tussock, the pingao and the washed wood that covered the beach like ghosts of horses. But I didn't keep my watch.

I've wondered since what it was that was working in me that day, taking my thoughts, turning me to different tasks. I shifted the stones of our outside fireplace and made a small fire so that I could melt lead scraps for sinkers. I was making moulds in the ground, shaping them with a thin knife, when Peka the perching seagull came down to the verandah ledge. I stopped what I was doing to talk to her, then I tried to sing her away. She fluffed herself and squawked, moved from foot to foot, and stayed. 'Get yourself off,' I said. 'You've got no business here,' which is no way to talk to Peka.

It was no way to talk to the one, who on cloudy mornings in the days when we mustered sheep on the hills, would wing back and forth, a shadow in the mist at the clifftops, keeping us back from the edge; who swooped back and forth in front of my horse when I contemplated the full river; who sat and watched with us while the old ones or the sick ones took to the old paths. I didn't say at those times, 'Go on your way, you've no business here.'

Forebearing bird. There was something at work that day. Perhaps I had given too much of myself, had stayed awake too long chanting in the dark, given too much and allowed myself to weaken.

Hopper came out pulling a cushion.

'You've nothing to tell me,' I said to Peka, because there was some strange thing working in me at that time, claiming me.

Then Peka lifted herself, squealed close by my head and flew down to the sea. So I took Hopper on my back and followed.

The sea was dense and quiet. I saw Tia swimming out over the flat deep water, sorrow making her careless. She was already on Whai's step and there was nothing we could do. There was no use in any of us going after her to knock at Whai's green door because he will always take in whoever comes and there is no return.

I think she stayed there and lived with Whai after that because we never found her though we watched the sea and searched the shores. But from Whai's place sometimes she would return. Often at night I'd wake and watch her walk through the rooms, stop and stand by Hopper's bed. 'Go on your way,' I'd say. 'You found your own path. You took yourself there, so now keep on going and go alone.' It was the only way to speak to her.

That was before the dust, before the mud, before the roads and the logging trucks. It was before the people went and before Hopper and I moved to the hard place out of the way of the machines.

I thought Peka might leave us after the people had gone, when we moved from the old place to the hard place, but she didn't. Peka was there when the hills began to tumble and when the river rose and broke out across the flats and climbed the higher ground because, far back in the hills, the trees had been trucked away. And Whai still rode with my Tia out in the bay.

When Hopper was seven, my daughters and their families came again. 'You'd better come now,' they said. 'So Hopper can go to school, and before the machines come this way.'

'I am his school,' I said. 'And the machines won't come here. No one wants a hard place without water where nothing grows.' But I knew the machines could go anywhere. I knew water could be made to go anywhere. 'We can't leave Peka and Tia and Whai.'

'Things are different now,' they said, but they went home.

Those were the days of dust after the ground had been scraped clean. The winds stirred the dust, the big trucks rolled through it. It settled everywhere on the house of the fish, the old tree, the woodstack, the tracks. Our eyes watered from it.

But when the rain came the dust turned to mud, the banks became streaked with furrows, the river broke and we were cut off by water. Even so we still had a way of getting to the sea.

There were other houses by now, with fences round them, shops and garages and places of accommodation. There were new people who played in the sea. They spoke to us sometimes. Sometimes we gave them fish. There were signs and flags now, boats and buoys and people playing.

A letter came to say the machines would soon come. All round us there was shouting and noise and I could see that the hard place would go. There had to be more places for the new people and their playthings. 'Where will Peka be?' I asked. 'If we go, where will Peka be?'

'Wherever we are,' Hopper said.

My daughters and their husbands came back again.

'You have to come now,' they said. 'Next week the bulldozers arrive.'

'What about Tia?' I asked.

'She's gone, taken the old road.'

'And Whai? Is he a red flag now, an orange buoy, a light on a pole?' No one answered me.

As we left I looked towards the tree, the tangled wood, the hut with the eye on the door. 'Burn it,' I said. So they did.

We watched it burn, jewelled, then we went, taking with us Peka, Whai, Tia and the House of the Fish, all of which live for as long as they stand in memory.

The Day of the Egg

Dorothy went to the fridge and took out an egg, holding it between the tips of three fingers and thumb. She was going to cook it with a slice of bacon and a few chips for the old man who she could hear in the bathroom watering his face. And when she came in she was going to tell him. The cat in the tree was the last thing.

Sam was a mate of her father's whom Dorothy had known since she was eight. It was usually on a Friday night that Sam would arrive with her father, both of them primed. They'd bring beer and pigs' heads and spend the weekend boozing. Not just the two of them. In the end there'd be a crowd. Dorothy and her brothers and sisters would go to sleep listening to the songs running into one another, the feet thumping, the uke and mandolin going to town, the teaspoon ringing in the neck of a bottle, the big spoons clacking. Now and then in the middle of the night there'd be a row, shouting and a scuffle, someone going headlong out the door.

In the morning the kitchen would be sour-smelling, and there'd be an array of sleeping bodies — one or two seated at the table with their heads among the bottles, glasses and cigarette ash, another stretched out on the kitchen settee, sometimes one or two on the floor.

Dorothy and her brothers and sisters would start cleaning up and eventually the sleepers would get up and go outside — find a way home, or prop themselves against a tree ready to start drinking again.

The kids would clear the table first, then get themselves Weetbix and hot water. They'd find the tin of condensed milk and dribble that over their Weetbix. If there was no Weetbix they'd make a drink with the condensed milk instead.

After breakfast they'd take all the bottles out and stack them behind the shed, make a fire for the rubbish, wash the glasses and dishes and floors. Their mother would get up eventually and come out into the kitchen croaky and sore, shiny from a cold-water wash. They knew she wouldn't say anything about the tin of condensed milk. Their father would go out to the wash-house to see if he'd remembered to hide a flagon or two there.

On Sunday afternoons Sam would go home to his wife and daughters, that is until his wife and daughters put his belongings out on the footpath one Sunday and locked the door. After that he came to live in an army hut on a farm property nearby.

Dorothy left home when she was seventeen and found work in a pharmacy in the city. When she was twenty she married a pharmacist called Phil.

Dorothy and Phil had been married for ten years and had two children when Dorothy's father died and her mother asked them to come and live in the house with her. In fact her mother wanted to give them the house as long as she could live there too — she and her cat, for the rest of their days. Dorothy talked to Phil who jumped at the chance of taking ownership of a freehold house, while at the same time hoping he wouldn't have to spend too much money doing it up. It was a bit of a dump. They did some renovations and moved in.

It was a morose, unattractive cat that Dorothy's mother had attached to herself. It was a square-faced tabby tom with chewed ears that put its stink all through the house. Phil thought of bringing it home a pill. It wasn't just that it was ugly, stinking and bad-tempered, but also it ate too much according to him.

Ever since Sam had come to live in the hut nearby, Dorothy's mother had done his washing, which she would go and collect from him once a week. In return he would chop and stack wood. Usually when her mother returned the clothes to him she'd stay and have a whisky because Sam liked the company, but apart from that her mother had given up drink. Her father, while he was alive, had toned his drinking down too over the years, even though he still went on a bender once in a while.

Sam, on the other hand, had stepped up his intake. After his retirement he would get up each day at six, walk across to the yard and work on the wood for an hour, then he'd fill his bucket with water, which was as much as he needed for the day, make himself a cup of tea and tidy his hut. At nine he'd be on the road with his bag over his shoulder, walking the four kilometres to the local. He'd return at four, pickled, with a bottle in his swag to keep him company for the night. Dorothy's mother and father worried about his habit of smoking in bed.

And one night the hut did go up in flames, but Sam managed to get out with a few minor burns.

After the fire, Dorothy's parents wanted Sam to come and live with them, but all Sam wanted was to move into the old wash-house, which is where he had often bunked down in the old days. So they fixed the wash-house up for him and life went on much the same as it had before, except that Dorothy's mother would go out each night before she went to bed to check that Sam had put his cigarette out before going to sleep.

It was soon after Dorothy and Phil moved into the house that Sam started seeing spiders. These were as big as plates and came out of the walls at him, or if he tried to escape outside they dropped down on him out of the bushes. Dorothy and Phil would hear him yelling, fighting them off out in his bunkhouse or crashing about yelling in the trees. At first Dorothy's mother tried to help him but soon found there was nothing she could do, so she left him to it. But every morning she'd cook him breakfast and make sure he ate it. Breakfast was his one meal of the day.

So when Dorothy's mother died, Dorothy and Phil inherited the house, the unfavoured cat, and Sam. At about that time too, Dorothy gave birth to an unplanned daughter, whose conception Phil had been sour about, wondering how it was that Dorothy, wife of a pharmacist, could have been so careless and so stupid.

The cat never came into the house once Dorothy's mother had gone. It went wild and at night they'd hear it growling and howling out in the trees.

Not long after Dorothy's mother's death Phil began to talk about Sam being moved. It wasn't the deetees he objected to, although that did come into the discussion. It wasn't the fact that Sam messed himself now and again or wet the bed, because that was Dorothy's problem. If she wanted to clean up those sorts of stinks it was up to her. What Phil objected to was the price of breakfast.

In truth Dorothy was disgusted with Sam too, sick of cleaning him up, sick of his smell, sick of his dingbats. She knew that the kids were ashamed of having someone like that around, and that Sam was the reason they never brought friends home to play.

'But he's got nowhere else to go,' Dorothy said.

'There's the Savvies,' said Phil. 'We'll drop him off at the Savs. He's just a freeloader. Everything goes on the booze. Nothing for Muggins.' Then he changed his voice to a sing-song squeak, 'Nothing for Muggins but Muggins does him a breakfast every morning.' Actually Dorothy was sick of Phil too.

It was when she found the cat hanging in the tree out by the wash-house with Sam's belt round its neck that Dorothy knew Sam would have to go. She took the cat down from the tree and buried it before the children got up, and when she went back into the kitchen and told Phil he delivered an ultimatum. 'Get him out of here,' he said, 'or I'm off. Have something arranged by the time I get home tonight, or that's it, I'm going, you can pack my bags.' Then he went out the door and Dorothy held her breath until she heard him backing the car down the drive. Then she let her breath go, slowly, thinking about what she would say to Sam, which words to use to tell him.

When she heard Sam coming she went to the fridge and took out the egg, and as he came in she turned towards the stove where the pan was heating. With her back to him it was easier to start talking.

'Uncle Sam, there's something important we have to talk about,' she said.

Then she dropped the egg.

And there was the egg staring up at her from the middle of a polyurethaned cork tile. The broken shell of the egg had distanced itself, standing off like a misshapen eyebrow. For a moment she looked at it, thinking about what it might be staring at, what it could be seeing — like herself standing above it, looking down, one hand poised holding a tight space between fingers and a thumb, lips parted ready for speech, prepared for an outflow of words that were important.

It was seeing Jenny, stopped in the doorway with Neddy behind, their eyes moving from her face to the floor and back again. It was taking in baby Harriet who was crawling quickly from under the table, laughing, reaching a fat finger to poke. It was seeing Sam with his hand on the door handle and the door half closed. The hand was bluish and flaky and had the shakes. Sam's face, turned towards her words and the sound of her voice, was frightened, the lower jaw was hanging and dribbly, and the bottom lids of his eyes had turned inside out and were meatish-looking.

Then Dorothy put her lips together, turned and reached for

a paper towel. Jenny and Neddy came in asking questions and laughing, the baby poked the egg–eye and smacked a spread hand down on the shell eyebrow. Sam finished shutting the door, turned with his shoulders hunched forward and his hands loose by his sides and said, 'What, Dotty?'

But her words, the carefully thought–out words, the words of importance, had been cut off, swallowed, under, or over, the stare of the egg. And during the process the words had changed and become other words.

She finished cleaning up, turned the pan off and shifted it from the element, pushed muesli under the noses of the two older children, picked up the baby and sat down.

'What, Dotty?' he said again.

'Phil's leaving,' said her changed words. 'Tonight after work. I'm moving you into Mum and Dad's old room. It's no good someone your age, someone sick like you, sleeping out in a dump of a shed. Actually I'm having that shed pulled down,' she said, though she'd only just thought of it.

She stood, shifting Harriet on to her hip where she felt as light as could be, flipped the stove switch, shifted the pan across.

'So that's it. All I have to do is pack his things, after I've made us some breakfast.'

The Sky People

There's a hole in the sky. Pierced. Where I could go, falling, falling, to a shimmering of colourful snow coming down in paper diamonds and triangles, as they do at the end of television quiz shows, hosts and contestants waving, smiling through them, while words slide upward.

Celebratory and welcoming these inside-the-sky snow-coloured fallings. I could be there in the real place of sky, feeling the soft shapes touch, then heap round me as I stand. And I could walk, lifting my legs high, turning my arms, watching the colours lift and swirl for me.

The sky child. I could search for him. It could be a happy journey.

I was happy once looking at a taupata tree. Shiny, as though each leaf could have been glycerined. The sun's light on the tree picked out the veins of each leaf, boldly, and the tree was being mine, showing itself to me. Nothing against me looking at it with my different eyes. Some leaves turned to cast light, others to cast shadow, hiding clusters of tiny green berries edged together, tender, like first teeth.

Allowing touch, if I wanted, but I didn't. I already knew the greenness, the cool, so why touch? But where it pulled its cool greenness from was difficult to know in such a desert place.

Looking through the underside of a leaf I saw that there was a fly silhouetted, warming or cooling itself, rubbing feet together in a miserly way. A fly could alight, could touch, I would not. But I was happy for that moment. So happy I could have jumped

in with an axe, chopped the whole thing down. If I'd touched.
   What touching can do.

'Sitting in corners, eating, chewing bones. Evil, evil,' I would hear my mother say. 'Eating, eating but skinny as rope. Why? Because she's feeding something. That's how you know there's something inside that's evil. Something eating, eating in her. And her, eating, eating — so bad we have to hide food, feeding something evil. Born like it, who knows why?

'Had to tie her to the bed when she was little, to keep her down. And somehow she dragged it. Tiny, tiny and she dragged it, the bed, across the room, getting strength from something inside, bad.

'Evil, no doubt at all, from when she was born. And from the time she was born there was a strawberry mark like a thumbprint on her head. And blood. A baby, just newborn, and yet there she was letting blood like a woman. I thought it then, and as she grew I knew.'

But there were others who called me darling, Trixie and Fan, who were my mother's sisters. 'Talking like that,' they would say to her, 'about your own daughter who's only a little girl.'

'Black and evil. It's not you who have to live with her,' my mother would say. 'Bad-eyed, gap-toothed, a mouth so big there's room for other teeth, room for another whole set in between. How do I know she won't witch me? How do I know she won't take to me? With a bread knife, an axe, a pan of hot fat, coming in at doorways evilling me.'

'It's yourself, yourself,' they'd say. 'Marrying a white man and having three fair children. Getting above yourself. The three fair ones, then her, the black one.'

'They're good children my Mary, my Jenny, my John. They're pretty and well mannered. But her? Cooking up who knows what. Boiling with evil and lies. How do I know she won't one day, with

an axe or a knife, take to me. Talking, talking, to no one, lips
moving, eyes going funny until I slap her. I crack her, try my
best to slap it out of her. Who knows what evil she's hatching?'

'It's you who's evil, beating her, screaming. He made you
silly, that flash husband of yours.'

It was Biddy, Diddy and Kiddy that she was talking about
that I talked to, children that none of them could see but who
came to play with me, and who I would talk to all day long. I
didn't know, when I was very young, who were and who were
not, until bruises helped my understanding. But I learned to
talk and play secretly, and to hold Biddy, Diddy and Kiddy as
treasure for myself in the mind of my heart.

But also there was an old man who talked to me, who listened
to me. Really. He was real. He'd come to my window, tap, tap
with a stick. 'Come away with me,' he'd say. 'Get me away from
these faceless ones, gone in the ears and eyes. There's a place.
Get me there, only you, you're the only one for me.' I thought
he was my grandfather sitting by my window in his pretty shirts,
talking and listening to me.

There was a teacher who would speak to me too. Oh, he wore
ties of stars, flowers, eyes, paint splashes, comic cats and frogs
and dogs. His hair was plastered down and he was pimply and
grey-eyed. 'Clever,' he would say to me. 'Good. Good girl.' I
wrote pages and pages every school day for him. I read book after
book for him. But then I told. 'It's difficult for me to know,' I
said one day to his grey eyes, 'who is or isn't. They talk to me.'

'Oh, oh well,' he said.

But he asked Mary, Jenny and John about Biddy, Diddy and
Kiddy and they hit me going home. Called me crackers, you're
evil you. And told. It was coming towards Christmas and the
pohutukawa tree out on the road was sitting ready with pale
buds, but overcome still with dark leaves. 'Get out, get out,
you're evil you, Devil's Eyes,' my mother said.

So there I was out on the old road but there was nowhere for me to go except to the tree. I twined myself in it. Watched from there. Fixed my upended eyes. And it made her afraid watching me watch her from between the ravelled branches.

So afraid that after two days she made me come back in.

After that there was a plot in the mind of her heart, though perhaps the plot had been in the mind of her heart from the time I came, thin and dark, from out of her. Perhaps we eyed each other then. She could've easily done then what was now in her heart and mind.

Each night, when she thought me asleep, the door of my room would open and she would step in with footfalls so light she must have known I would hear, thoughts so loud she must've known I would know them.

One night she came right in and I smelled the killing odours of her, grey and dense, flowing from her like ghostly rivers, fetid streams. I was fixed to the ledge that was my bed, letting her come. Who would know in the morning? Who would mourn in the knowing?

Towards me reeking, with a heavy pillow. But she was too afraid of thin, muscled arms, gaps between teeth, my vertical eyes. I kept them closed, letting her come. Right beside, holding the pillow, frightful. Then she backed away and never tried again. Frightfilled.

So she couldn't kill me. Or even turn me out onto the ditchy road. That's when I understood, knew, my power — when my
Mother

Tried to

Kill me

But didn't

Because of what I

Might do

To her

From then on I had true use of my power. I would speak in any voice. I would evil my sideways eyes, rolling the whites of them forward while standing with my arms extended. I would walk without sound, sit without breathing. I would talk when I wanted to talk — or use my silence, grasping the power of my spaced-out teeth, my meeting eyebrows, my wrong way, upslid eyes.

And in two months she was dead.

Her fright had killed her. Walking backwards from my room with the pillow, had killed her. My voice, my silence, my breath had killed her.

I left, so glad to have killed, going out onto the old tree road. Old Man, old Grandfather was there with his sugarbag of bones, pissing in the ditch. 'Take me with you,' he said. 'We were meant for each other. I belong to you, you belong to me,' as in the words of songs.

'There's a place where we could go,' he said, cocking his head, eyeing the sky. 'If you take me there.'

'I've got powers,' I told him as we walked away together.

'You lose them if you talk like that,' is what he said.

'They're not bones in the bag,' he said to me when I told him to leave the bag behind. 'It's just what they say, the ones without faces, no ears and no eyes. In here's what I need — a knife, a cup, a cloth, pictures, shirts, a few things for me, waiting for you. Two of us.'

Then I knew it was right for us to be together. I took his hand. 'Am I your granddaughter, your helper, your companion or your wife?' I asked.

'My grandmother,' he said. 'I've got the photo in my bag.'

On the train I found him a seat by the window, put his bag and his cap on the hook, as a grandmother would do. But then I reached the bag down again. 'The picture of me, your grand-mother.'

He loosened the drawstring of the bone bag and took out an

old photograph of a young woman sitting on a step smiling, showing her spread apart teeth, squinting her slope-away eyes. Me, but white-skinned, brown-haired.

'Did she have powers?' I asked.

He thought about that.

'I think she lost them,' he said, which made my heart beat hard.

'How? How? Tell me.'

'Or gave them away.'

He took the photo from me while my heart jolted, and turned his sky-eye to the window. After a while he turned back to me. 'And then you got them back,' he said. 'Caught them. From her.' So I moved close to him, put my arm through his and leaned my head against my dear old child.

When he went to sleep I switched on my perpendiculars, put on my gappy-toothed smile, to work my powers. Some people nodded my way going by in the carriage, some smiled or spoke. Some looked and turned away, but none ignored me. No one walked by without hesitation.

Almost at the end of the journey Helene came in, swinging on to the seat beside her a brown velvet bag. 'Thank God, or whoever,' she said.

She had tangerine hair, brown lipstick and blusher, brown eye shadow and eyeliner, eyebrows pencilled in brown, a bundle of copper triangles hanging from one ear. She wore a yellow T-shirt that had been cut up and tasselled, the smallest of brown velvet skirts pricked with badges, gold tights and gold plastic shoes. She was round and blue-eyed with fat freckled arms.

'I nearly missed,' she said, sitting, clacking the badges.

I flicked at her, gapped. 'I saw you running.'

'From lost causes, visiting parents,' she said. 'Is that your parent there?'

'He said I'm his grandmother,' I said.

'Dotty old loony. Gaga old coot.' She laughed and she looked like the queen of the world.

'The photo's in my bag,' he said, as though he had not just been asleep.

'We decided to run off together,' I said.

'From what?'

'From people without faces.'

'Gone eyes, gone ears.'

'Far out,' she said. I couldn't get over watching her laugh and smile.

'My name's Helene,' she said. 'That's what they gave me, what they wanted me to be — pastel and bows, tutu and flute, arabesque and point.' Tossing tangerine. 'We live in a warehouse, Baker, his kid and I. Baker and I are lovers. We make clothes. He's indigenous, tangata Maori, like you,' and she laughed and smiled. 'And the band stays Friday to Sunday. There are no wares now, in the warehouse. Just two ginormous rooms and a row of ex-offices at the top of some stairs, that are too shabby for the owners to lease to businesses and too expensive for them to upgrade. So I guess they're glad of us and what we can pay. There's a big stack of shelves in one of the rooms. That's where the band sleeps.'

'I'm Nina. I'm used to sleeping on shelves,' I said.

'You could unpick and iron, be our model.'

'What about him, my grandchild, looking for a place in the sky?'

'Jewellery,' she said.

We were pushing one behind the other into wind. Helene, the queen of the world, laughing, shoes in hand, tassels and bag tugging and flapping; me, laughing too, slitting my verticals into grit and fumes; Skyfinder and his bag of bones behind, calling,

'Jewel, hey Jewel, I think you are my sister.' Tickets, wrappers and packets spinning, drink can slewing away.

Walking alongside us was a building of old brick and painted-over windows. Dang, dang, dang, went Jewel on the downpipes with the shoes. Drrr drrr went the shoes on iron railings of the wharf gates. In the gateway Jewel turned and extended her arms out to flowers at each side. 'Agapanthas,' she said, white and blue like her skin and eyes. Her orange hair shooshed forward. Arabesque, she did, and point, arched. Agapanth and point. Then bowed, turned, went through the gates.

So I did it too. Turned, arabesqued my best, pointed, out-armed and bowed, hair flapping forward. Skyfinder's palmy lagoon shirt had unbuttoned and he was full sail into the wind. 'Agapanthas,' he turned and called to cars sliding, trucks barking, motorbikes pop-popping up to red lights. Agapanthas and bow.

'Beware of Propeller' my squeezed slanters saw on the *Pacifica* with its end open and loads going in. 'Takeaways' said a hole in a wall. The water rocking and slapping amongst the jetties was greenstone and heliotrope — rocking and slapping a black-backed gull, a brown bottle, a brown duck. And was looked into by hooded statues. Hunched, one of them drew up out of it a white fish.

Kiosks, containers, giant brick and concrete sheds with giant painted words ART and KEEP CLEAR on giant doors. Insect cranes stood above them.

There were *Wakakura*, *Betsy O'Ryan*, *Makepeace*, *Juno*, a smell of fish, flags for everything rap rapping.

There were rows and rows of cars boxed in against hoardings —ⁿɒƨƨiᴎ lidoM ⁿɒƨƨiᴎ lidoM ⁿɒƨƨiᴎ lidoM — walking backwards alongside. Sweep, my skewed eyes went, to buildings leaning back against hills — buildings of blue, black, silver, green and gold glass. Daytime lights pricked high in them like stars.

Up, up, up, there was a white plane pulling itself into a dense sky.

'We Win,' a billboard declared, wind chopping us sideways as we upstepped onto an over-ramp and walked above traffic booming like drums. Then down and out onto footpaths, in and out amongst the people leaning, holding against themselves, against ourselves, clothes, bags, our lives. We waited together at the crossing. 'Cross, Wait, Wait, Wait,' the lights winkered as we went, finding our line again one behind the other.

Until we were in a doorway, rigged against the dark walls of it while we breathed. 'This is it,' said the Jewel of the world, jinking her bag for the sound of keys then fishing them out. 'Up there,' pointing as we followed her through, 'there's a printing outfit on the bottom floor, after that upupupupup, then us, up there.'

There were our three heads dropped back, dividing a circle into thirds, chins almost touching as we stared up, down a well with a pink ceiling at the bottom of it, stairs whorling up and round, descending into it.

The circle broke and we were in line again, Jewel with her shoes on now, tap tapping on the stairs, me in step and two steps behind, Skyfinder two down, in step behind.

'We're not allowed to live here of course, of course,' said Jewel's voice from off the walls of yellow, pink and purple, Alkeen, Ray May, Through to Bengal Tiger. 'It's supposed to be be storerooms, studio studio, headquarters quarters for the band the band the band.'

'Hey Jewelewel, don't make it ba-a-a-ad,' called Skyfinder.

'But they turn a blind eyeeyeeyeeye.'

'Take a sa-ad songsong and make it be-e-e-der,' I sang.

Ba-a-a-ad, eyeeyeeye and song and song and be-e-e-der, be afrai-ai-afrai-ai, ha ha, ha ha, let her let her, un-under yoursk in-in-in, ha ha,

Ha ha,
Ha ha ha ha,
Ha ha ha ha ha ha,
Ha ha ha ha ha ha ha ha, as we untwined the stairs.

Close to the pink ceiling Jewel fitted a key into a new door. 'Hel and Bak' the door said, 'and Steffy' it said in brackets lower down. Opened, stepped in, and we were in the sky.

We entered a passageway with boarded-over windows along one side, paste-ups on the other which told me I should save the world and I could do anything. 'I know it,' I said. 'Mine is the power, in my great teeth mouth and my spying turn-upped eyes.'

'Where have you been, Hel?' a biscuity girl wearing curtains, standing in sky, called from the end of the funnel.

'Steffy, we've got new friends.'

'I'll tell Baker then.'

'I used to be a bathroom consultant, which came about from me being good at art at school,' said Baker over coffee in a jar. Studebaker Renata was his name. 'Scooting about in the firm's well-dressed van with my colour charts, formica, tile and wall-paper samples, shiny pictures of baths, showers, spas, loos and accessories. My décor books, my big mouth yabbing advice on mirrors, skylight, one-way windows, the hiding of toothbrushes, the displaying of fat, toning towels. The people it was who consulted, not the bathrooms, but I'd just as soon it was bath-rooms — I need implants, man, for cosiness, explants for space. I want lights, man, I want to be a fairground. I need love. What can be done about the undercover or coverover odours of me, what to do about pubes in the tubes?

'Until the bathroomer had an affair with a bathroomee. It was bathroom boredom that did it. Hers and mine. For her it was the last place. She'd done over the living areas and the laundry. The kitchen and dining rooms had been extended and

74

rehashed. The bedrooms had had all the kiddie stuff removed and been luxurified. She'd had a vertical designer tank of tropical fish installed in the hallway, a picture window in the kitchen, and a conservatory built on for indoor-outdoor living. Then came the psychologist to bathrooms. Me. Bringing a boredom big enough to match hers.

'I would wonder how a dentist felt looking in a different mouth of teeth every twenty minutes, picking and poking in cavities, slops, build-ups, breath. Those big bad mouth bathroom slops, cavities, breaths, build-ups were getting me down. We got down to it together, bathroomer and bathroomee.

'But we couldn't be -er and -ee after that, or at least she couldn't be -ee to me, she preferred what she had after all. But I'm grateful to her because she kept Steffy for me.

'It was no go for a bathroomer to go round with a squeaky package strapped against his chest, stretch-and-grow legs dangling about his midriff. I got my marching orders. Ex-bathroomer went on DPB and into high fashion as a sideline.'

'Now we are beloveds,' Jewel said.

'I'm part of her rebellion, being wrong-aged, wrong-coloured, jobless, so to speak.'

'One day, my parents are convinced, I'll come to my senses, dress properly, marry a banker. Or even a correctly toned young bathroomer would have done, I believe . . . Who are you today, Steffy?'

'The witch's assistant.'

'What do you do?'

'Make birthday cakes for witches, do unmagic, that sort of stuff.'

There it was, the witch's cake, a mound of green velvet and pink lace, studded with diamonds.

I was the only one drinking coffee from a jar. Jewel and Baker had brown mugs, Steffy had a sailing ship cup and Skyfinder had a picnic tumbler from out of his bag of bones. 'On Saturday there are markets,' Jewel said. 'Paddy's, Quay and Flea. But tomorrow? Definitely Flea. For a cup and plate each, or whatever you need to eat and drink out of or from, or with. And something to sleep on. Foam. Sheets and covers we make on our magic machine.'

From the morning windows the grey southerly was still scrummaging amongst green-black, purple-brown, charcoal-white of sea, hills and sky. Beating together. Wild water, seabirds blowing. Hills on their haunches could have stepped up, bared teeth, come at each other head on. Or could have stood back and howled together at the flying sky where we were. There were houses climbing the old hills, and buildings with their weekend eyes closed. We went down the shouting stairs and out.

We were eating mutton, watercress and doughboys along with truck drivers stopped for fleamarket breakfast, trucks still revving on the side. Fritters and sausages were laid out too, chop suey, chow mein, doughnuts, bread and tea. Wind slapped round big bare legs of truck drivers, wagons of fruit and vegetables, tables of secondhand clothes and shoes and goods, cakes and sweets, plants and books, doll and poodle toilet-roll covers. Hot dog and toffee apple boy called, 'Hey nice big one for you Steffy you got a dollar, and the wind been sticking things on my toffee apples.'

'What we do,' said Jewel, 'is buy from the fleamarket, make whatever into whatever, then sell it at our stall in the Quay. Today I do Flea, Baker does Quay.'

'Buy at the Flea, sell at the Quay,' sang draped Steffy.

'Anything,' said Jewel. 'Cotton, linen, leather, bark, wool, coconut, copper, wire, sticks, shells, nuts and nails. Or we find stuff in skips. Scrounge.'

Jewel bought a pink fan-pattern knitted stole for fifty cents, a linen suit for a dollar, lacy blouse and velvet jacket for twenty each; a feather duster, red plastic ribbon, a card of buttons, a bundle of zips — the lot a dollar. 'We saved them for you, Helly,' said the legwarmered stallkeepers.

'We met here at the fleamarket, Baker and me,' said Jewel. 'It wasn't love at first sight — him eating mutton and puha, interested in the crushed velvet skirts and waistcoats that were in fashion then, that I was selling, telling me his mouthful of ideas, Steffy by the hand. After that he brought drawings. "Remodel, renovate," he said, in bathroom psychology language, and we'd talk and talk long after the stalls had gone leaving the car park free for "proper" nine o'clock Saturday shopping.

'Not until afterwards, when I got this place to work in, did we think of it. We each had our own downtown, rundown flats that we couldn't afford. We thought of working up top and living there together. Also, "We could get it on," we said with eagerness and almost together in the middle of fun-fur rompers, appliquéd. So we did, became beloveds.'

I bought a plate on which a cobblestone path led through flowers and shrubbery to a thatched cottage, then on to a green gate beyond which was a yellow hedge and autumny trees. 'A bit Of Old England' the words said. The shape of the plate put this whole scene into blue-edged parentheses. I bought a heavy white cup with half a handle, a knife, a fork, a spoon, and a roll of foam good enough for mattresses for Skyfinder and me.

'Tally Ho' was what his plate was about — six pink huntsmen and their horses, twenty-one dogs, a woman at a cottage door too far distant for a proper face, although there were two tiny dots of eyes, enough for her to see the huntsmen with. There was enough of a hand for her to wave goodbye to them.

Somewhere, somewhere, hiding in a hole in the peppermint-coloured hills, or creeping through the peppermint trees, would be the fox. 'Fields of green,' my old child said. 'And skies of blue,' as he peered and peered with his sky eye.

Afterwards he found for himself a red hibiscus shirt. In the wind. One by one the trucks brrrmming away, and suddenly the food and goods and the flapping stands and wrapped-up people were gone and we went chattering home.

'One of those armchair ones,' said Jewel, showing me her bed, pulling the covers off, then flipping it back into place to be a chair. 'Put the covers out of sight and it's my pattern room, my wardrobe room, with its own good chair. All my own clothes hanging up, ticketed and labelled ready for market. And my long table where I draw the patterns out.

'Steffy's got a settee to sleep on,' she said, showing me. 'And we keep in here the unpicked lace, buttons, zips and things. And kiddy clothes. The room between hers and mine can be yours, but it's full of junk, pinex and gib, from a wall we pulled down. And Skyfinder, opposite, can clear cardboard boxes from one end of the jewellery room.'

I couldn't stop watching her laughing and putting out her arms. I used some of Skyfinder's words. 'I think you are my sister,' I said.

'Your opposite twin,' she said.

All day Skyfinder and I cleared and cleaned our rooms while Jewel whipped up sheets and covers of a thousand colours for us on her sewing machine, undid a bean bag to make pillows, while in and out, upstairs, downstairs, in black clothes and sunglasses, came and went members of the band.

Came and went the bedecked witch's assistant with messages: 'Helly's making coffee now. Jossy and Jessie's kissing on the stairs. I wrapped a parcel once, when I was four, and left it by the window for the witch to find and when I woke up it was gone. In it was bottletops, a cat picture, a candle from my birthday. Jeanette from the standard class asked if I'm an alternative lifestyler. "I'm a flowermaker," I said. I wasn't a witch's assistant then. "You're cute," said Jeanette. Skyfinder said that I'm an angel so I'm going to look for the clothes.'

There it was, my room, once it was empty. Waist-high partitions with glass above — dirty glass, cracked glass, some panes painted over. And a floor of was-green Feltex with tripping edges and corners. A cosy corner for my bright-covered mattress, my patchwork sheet, my overlocked blanket made of jerseys, coats and cardigans. Pinex dust and gib bits. My own blue door.

Through a darkroom, used by photographers on weekdays, was a door into a room with a showerbox up a ladder, rigged there by ex-bathroomer, Baker. At the end of a corridor, rigged to fill from a handbasin and to run off into a urinal, was a washing machine. Next to it were loos with brass catches that slid across to show vacant or engaged. Out in the big room, in the corner, was a Zip water heater over a sink beside a red refrigerator. 'All the gears,' said Jewel.

And there was Skyfinder across the way, knocking down shelves to make himself a bed which would be hidden by a screen of pinned jewellery. Shelves of hooks and clasps and pins, buttons and sticks and beads, coins and copper, shell and feathers, plastic and perspex and glass, wire and cardboard, paint and dye. 'It's here,' he happily said, 'with a grandmother, a sister, a brother, an angel. It's here, where the birds are, where they come and bring their findings to the sky.'

'Can you make earrings, brooches and things?'

'For angels,' he said.

We had fifteen dollars' worth of fish and chips, Jewel, Baker, Steffy, Skyfinder, the band and I. We undid the parcel, spreading it on the mat in the big room and sat in a circle around. About the papers' edges were a bag of bread, a dish of butter, bottles of sauce and vinegar. Himona, Ra, Setu, Fetu, Jossie, Jessie, Kataraina and Ihaia were the band who had inned and outed, upped and downed all afternoon, transferring gears to the gig place downtown.

'What are you known for?' one of them asked.

'Evil,' I said, flickering my sideways eyes about the circle through the steam. 'Murder,' I said.

'Faar out.'

'Fuck me dayz.'

'I told you,' said Jewel with joy.

'Who did you murder?'

'My mother.'

'Really?'

'Really,' said Jewel.

'Really really really?'

'Really really really.'

'Really really really really really really really?'

'Really really really really really really really.'

'How?'

'With bad eye,' I said. 'With staring not breathing, chewing inanimate objects, with shaving a part of my head up to the strawberry thumbprint, with talking to Biddy, Diddy and Kiddy in silent tones, with letting her do herself in.'

They all watched me, listened to me, eyes and ears about the circle, but I wasn't the only one talking. Mine wasn't the only voice. Two away from me there was Skyfinder, saying, 'It goes, it goes, if you treat it like that. It's how she lost it I think, by talking too much. She lost it. And then you got them back again, from her. They'll go, treating them like that.'

'What are you known for?' they asked Skyfinder.

'Searching,' he said. 'Searching everywhere. And for tropical shirts of hibiscus, red birds, coconut palms, dolphins and orange lagoons. Looking for my island in the sky with flowers made of paper warmly snowing. Looking for the eared and eyed.

'Once I was a dancer to drums. I was a watcher first, on Sundays. Then I was allowed to wear the pareu and the 'ei, and to dance. They taught me how, not mentioning that I danced so awkwardly. They liked, they said, to have amongst them an old Papa'a. But after a year or two it stopped, people left, died, found other things to do, taking with them their drums and flowers, their eyes and ears.'

It was true what Skyfinder said he could do — make for angels. In the weekends we went fleamarketing and garage sale-ing with Jewel or Baker. On week mornings Skyfinder would go out and about the streets, the jetties, the bays, finding. At lunch time he'd return to spread his scratchings along the long table, sorting, matching, cutting, colouring, spraypainting. There were no bits of anything that he couldn't stick together, nothing he couldn't fit with hooks or clasps or mountings.

There was no one like him for mismatching, and his creations, being so misfittingly and absurdly untuned, became marvellous.

'It gives me double concussion, all this unsymmetry and jarring of the brain,' Baker said.

I was so proud of my old grandson mulling over his peckings with no thought for cold or food or sleep. I had to mind him as a grandmother does — Jewel, Baker, Steffy having to be sister, brother, angel to him. There never was wacky jewellery like his wacky jewellery for witchy angels like Steffy, Jewel and me, or for the marketers who went booting or barefooting up the stairs, Fridays, Saturdays and Sundays to see what was next in Hel and Bak clothes, Skyfi earrings, necklaces, bracelets, badges and brooches, belt buckles, pins and clips for hair.

'All in white,' said Jewel, with an arm-out and bow, showing us the creations, 'is this outfit entitled New Zealand Maid. The yoke has been cut from a tablecloth of white vinyl and the neck and arm trims are clear plastic hosepipe. The bodice is a full, old-style corset and the skirt has been made from a triple layer of net strips, ex-tutu, caught up here and there with silk tassels from a skip shawl. The two cone-shaped springs at the bust line are from thief-proof petrol-tin caps and the front decorations are from glass necklaces and old chandeliers. Central to the back is this silver crucifix surrounded by bracelet charms and large pearls. To offset this garment there are the fringed marching-girl boots studded in silver, and this peaked hat of vinyl and white tubing.

'This strapless, mid-length evening gown has been cut from a blackout curtain from Clyde Quay School assembly hall. The skirt is distinguished by the many gold rubber snakes moving in every direction upon it. These are seen through the complete overlay of clear plastic. Accessories are snake tiara, earrings and anklets.

'Here we have a day dress, this time in brilliant green Astroturf on a long-waisted bodice of blue tarpaulin. The blue gauze carnations decorating the skirt have been retrieved from bridesmaid's headwear. Wear with it these colourful tennis shoes handpainted by Baker of Hel and Bak.

'This simple brown pinafore has been cut from an ocelot coat with thigh decorations of lampshade fringes in shades of maroon and gold. Front buttons are real and jenyuwine, off the rock mussel shells.

'"Rainy Day", with the layered look, has been created from black umbrellas left in trains, coffee bars, bus shelters, theatres, galleries all over Wellington — or which have been blown inside out by our refreshing Wellington winds and abandoned in gutters and rubbish bins. The hat has been devised from the frame of an umbrella and the earrings have been modelled from brolly handles.

'Here is our Kia Ora gown with its skirt of laminated Good Luck Kia Ora New Zealand coasters. To go with this we have a special cloak which we have called Lest We Forget. This fine garment has been decorated with one hundred plastic tikis from Air New Zealand, lest we forget, or lest Air New Zealand forget this recent and dishonourable time in their history. Some of the tiki have been reversed so logo and name can be picked out in pink highlighter for all to see, lest we forget. Interspersed among the one hundred tikis, and obtained from our airport and souvenir shops round town, are little bunches of pois, and Maori warrior rubbers with little drawn-on skirts and stick-on bulby, googly eyes. All edges have been trimmed in genuine, imitation taaniko ribbon. To complete this ensemble, here are two little Maori dolls made in Hong Kong. We have removed the headbands from their little fuzzy heads, removed the piupius from their little pot bellies and dressed them in pinstripe business suits, given them a little briefcase each, painted on shoes and put hooks in their heads so that they can be earrings.

'On to miscellaneous. Bright pink dress crocheted by Baker from fluorescent garden twine, partnered by a disco suit in silver vinyl. Canvas trenchcoat made from a sail, painted like zebras. Fun-fur jumpsuit in red. Shoe-velvet hats, necktie, jackets. Fish and animal handbags, flare jeans with inserts of American flag.

'And now let us present ta-ta-ra, our range of Skyfi jewellery? A banana pendant on a chain of red, blue, green and yellow plastic monkeys; clock face earrings with springs and glass beads; bunches of brightly coloured Lana Turner swizzle-stick earrings and matching pendants; necklets of dolls' limbs; earrings of heart-shaped biscuit cutters and medallions; green crab claws in the form of a cross on a big gold chain; teddy and fish-eye necklace; gold golfer, tennis player and footballer pendants from trophy stands; Barbie head earrings; bullet, sheep, kiwifruit, plastic golf ball and kewpie doll charm bracelets; earrings of House of Parliament coasters and little coloured flags.'

I was so happy living in the sky, caring for my dear grandchild, reminding him there was food, putting a shawl round his shoulders to keep him warm. I was happy having a mirror twin, a skin brother and an angel to complete my family. And I was happy showing the clothes and jewellery, witching people with my spacy teeth, my pitching eyes. 'Ahhh' and 'Oh' they said, and they called and clapped for me.

And I was in love for a while with Ihaia who was a stick insect who played drums. I magicked him, powered him until he came to me.

Sometimes Skyfinder, my dearest child, would fall asleep in the afternoons with his arms on the table of pickings and his head on his arm. Like a grandmother I would try to persuade him to lie down and sleep after lunch because I could see he was tired. Like a grandchild he would say he didn't want to go to sleep, as though if he slept he would miss something that was going on. But then his head would go down on his arm without him realising it, and he would sleep for an hour among the doll faces, cartridges, tubing, cable wire, advertisement coasters, paper clips, shells, beads, paper doilies, fridge magnets, safety pins, shards, ice-cream sticks, buckles, bows, buttons, zips, feathers, seeds, beads, chains, trick eyeballs, spiders, flies, hooks, studs, detergent bottles, hoops, switches, fittings, bells, toothbrushes, sheep, kiwifruit, tools and files, paints and glue.

One day he didn't wake up. We couldn't wake him and when we tried to move him he was shaped in against the table.

So we had to get him taken away and put in a coffin. Then we had to bring him back up the crying stairs in it, keeping him on the level. We had to unroll his mattress by the big sky windows, put the box on it and open it up ready for people to come and see him dressed so finely in his shirt of tropical birds and his sky cloth. In with him, by his arms, by his sides we tucked the items from his bone bag which were all the things he would need for his sky journey. The bag itself we folded and put under his feet. We wove a band of flowers for his head, and round his neck put a carved pig tusk on a string.

People came from off the streets and from markets, theatres, shops and studios all over town. The band played and we dressed up and paraded all the clothes and jewellery for him, all weekend.

After that we had to put the lid back on, do up the wing nuts as though we were preparing him for the magician to saw in half, or as though the little wings would fly him. We had to take him down the stairs, levelling him, then have him driven to the cemetery in a smooth grey car that looked as if it needed to be diminished and made into an earring.

We had to bury him while our clothes all pulled and tugged in the wind and the trees rattled and the clouds rolled about and the band played. Then we had to go and get pissed.

After that there we all were with him unseen amongst us. There we were talking to his unseen self — 'Hi Skyfinder,' 'Hey Skyfinder, tell me this and that,' 'Why is or isn't, Skyfinder, come on it's your favourite.' Living in the sky.

And there we were work, work, working late and early because by now we had contracts for theatres and shows, new customers coming every day, markets quickly expanding. We had to bring in new machinery, hire some sewers and let someone else run the market stall. We were so busy that I had no time for special powers, and no dear grandchild to remind me to feed them, practise them, not to treat them like this or like that, talk about them this way, that way.

'I didn't really mean us to make so much money,' said Jewel one day. 'I just wanted enough and a different life. But I couldn't help knowing how.'

'We want to live in a house now,' said Baker, 'with outside space and trees.'

'Tinted glass, barbecue, sane bathrooms,' I said to be difficult, pleased to see Jewel's eyes and mouth slide down.

'You too,' she said, 'if you want.'

'If, if,' I said.

'Come with us, or have your own house or flat, own-your-own, nearby.'

'Own, own.'

'Truly.'

'Truly, truly,' pleased to see almost tears.

'We have to change now in order to turn out all the stuff. Up here's no good any more if we want to keep on going, meet demands.'

'Demands, demands.'

'We have to be managers,' Baker said, 'of design.' He bowed. 'Of business,' Jewel bowed. 'Of presentation and sales,' arming-out to me. I couldn't help it, I bowed.

'And we might have a baby too,' Jewel said.

'Might have, might have,' I said to remind her she'd always had choices, to downcast her, punish her, power her because I didn't want my life to change. I was happy then with my opposite twin, my brother, my grandson's angel, and the unseen presence of him. I was happy with Ihaia and the band. In the sky place.

'We'll make this into a work area, offices and showroom, or might have to move everything closer to the ground. So there won't be room for any of us, or the band any more. And anyway it's not a place where we can invite . . .' Grandmothers, she was about to say but thought better of it. 'We want you to be happy,' she said.

'Want, want,' I said, being careful which words I selected to repeat.

'You're being an arsehole,' Baker said and I cut him with my slicers.

But my eye-slicing, powering, had no effect on Baker. I'd

talked too much, weakened myself, given too much away. There was still enough power in me to punish my Jewel, downcast her, cause her round blue eyes to turn themselves away from my witching verticals. Even so it was not enough to divert her from her plans.

'It's cool, no worries,' said the band to Jewel and Baker. 'We got a tour jacked up. North Island, then who knows? South Island? Ozland? Up RiZing's uprising,' they said with their fists in the air.

'You could come with us,' Ihaia said to me. But I knew I didn't want to give up the work I was doing to be an appendage to a band, like a silent instrument.

By way of punishing Jewel and Baker who bought a house with room enough for all of us, I down-deposited on an o.y.o. on the other side of town. A pretty carpeted unit with passion fruit walls and gas warmth upstairs and down was where I ensconced myself, exciting myself briefly by buying a baby fridge, a microwave, an automatic washing machine and a beautiful chair; exciting myself further by making cushions and curtains from ball gowns, bridesmaid outfits, sequins, shells, beads, peacock feathers and silk thread. Sitting in the tidy driveway was my pink van, announcing along its sides 'Hel and Bak with Nina'. I couldn't help but be pleased for a time.

However, there was now so much work that I was seldom in my own-your-own. I was finding markets for 'Hel and Bak' all over the country, soon extending to overseas markets. I seldom visited the skyhouse now. When I did go there I was an onlooker among the new makers and modellers. No more trying on, snapping my skinny hips, sparrow shoulders, tipsy eyes, parading the clothes. But I longed for that.

No more spinning up the steps of Quay Market with armloads of garments, boxes of accessories, hanging them, placing them, making big signs with fat marker pens. No more powering of market customers, reeling them in with my quirky eyes, step this way, snaring them with my powers and sending them away jingling and excited with their purchases. No more chatter, talk, talk, talk, from morning to night. My o.y.o. was just a container after all.

My other containers were the Hel and Bak with Nina van that took me round the city and its outskirts, aeroplanes that took me to other cities and other countries, hotel rooms and rooms of lovers that I did not love.

Silent times, in which I felt my powers ebbing, through lack of need, lack of use, and perhaps because I had earlier talked about them indiscriminately.

Contained, I was. Squeezed.

'We're going on holiday,' Jewel said over the phone one day. 'Baker and I, Steffy, Fleck and Rain. Good Friday until Tuesday. We want you to come.'

I should have sprung, but my sap was down. 'I can't,' I said. 'I'm buying a new house, a bigger place, with room to move.' It was something that came out of my mouth.

Since I'd said it I thought I should do it. I bought a house and moved into it in time to spend Easter in it alone. I spent the days going from window to window, looking out. On one side I looked out at sixty-four varieties of roses which could be watered by a system of discreet sprinklers that turned themselves off and on. On the other side were shrubs and outdoor furniture, and at the back were rockeries and garden ponds, and an embarrassed clothesline that did nothing to flaunt clothes.

Beyond were trees and a park where no one played. To the front was a wide, tree-lined street of large houses and multiple garages where no one walked and where cars moved quietly and slowly along.

Weekdays brought landscapers with instant gardens, builders adding and taking away, kitcheners, tilers, pavers, quoters, bathroomers. Everyone else an -ee who knew nothing of the -er of my life or self, or that I was happy once looking at leaves, happy once sky living.

Now I could neither capture nor enchant no matter how I turned my eyes. Gone.

Instead the eyes were on me — my face, my clothes, my Hel and Bak van — with the power to kill, because although avoided on pathways I was being evilled from behind doors. I could smell the killing odours of it.

No music aloud.

No shouting aloud.

No laughing aloud, singing aloud, screaming aloud.

Window to window.

Window to window to window.

Framed.

I thought of him, my grandchild, thought of following him. Thought of the place in the sky, colour snow in paper shapes falling, so gently heaping around, where I could be paperlight dancing, witching my elegant eyes.

So I dressed myself in New Zealand Maid — white vinyl, corset, tulle, petrol can springs, chandelier crystals, glass beads, silver bracelets and crucifix, which I had showed and modelled so many times that it had become my own. I clipped on the Skyfi medallion and earrings, put my feet into the marching-girl boots with the white roller blind fringes, flicking my wrists to do the lacing.

I dressed in my best for the hibiscus child whom we had sent to sky. I silvered my lips and my uphill eyes and thought about how I could find him, out-frame myself from.

Framed.

I stepped back from the largest window, long steps until my back was up against the furthest wall and from where I could see through the window, above trees, the lustrous sky.

Then I ran, flew, cracking, splintering, screaming through the window in a shower of white, silver and orange champagne with the sky coming nearer, nearer, and I was falling, falling, into it.

'I lost them,' said the words coming from the mouth of my stitched and bandaged head which was stitched to my stitched and bandaged body which was stitched to my splinted arms and legs.

'But I brought you your angel,' Jewel, holding a hand each of Fleck and Rain, said, 'who found them.'

'From talking too much at an earlier time, from not practising, forgetting, treating them like that.'

'We all do it, forget and lose. But your angel found them.'

'He told me, warned me.'

'She caught them. Now they're with her,' she said. 'I brought you your angel. She wants to come and live with you.'

So without shifting, I swivelled my one good upsidedown to Steffy who was grown and golden and woman-looking. She jingled her spangles, flashed at me her coppery diagonals, her witching teeth.

'Angel?' I asked.

'In a sky place,' she said. 'I was happy then.'

'And we'll be makers?'

'Of witches' pictures.'

'Pitchers?'

'Pictures. Pictures that seethe and writhe and flower, burst out crying and laughing. Covering every big up-in-the-sky wall from top to bottom and end to end. From found objects.'

'Founders.'

'Of pull-apart manikins, billboards, festoonery, glue bags, cat skulls, garments, cuttings and flags. Every flea and jumble, doorway, tidybin, alleyway, basement, opshop, swapshop, Sallyann.'

'Founders keepers.'

'Maori doll dancers with dance clothes removed, fitted out in costumes belonging to their other lives — factory and skivvy outfits, streetgirl and nightclub get-ups, drag doll, pin-up, wedding doll with supermarket trolley, housie queen. Covering a wall. And wild cakes too, elephant high, elephant wide.'

'With tattooed Maori chief candles for happy birthdays. Maybe China man fishing candles and breasted maiden candles too.'

'In high, wide rooms.'

'As soon as I'm realigned.'

'We'll hitch costumed Fleck and Rain to belts and pulleys. In and out and around it all they'll fly.'

'When it's ready, we'll light the candles, have a party in high clothes and all the singers and dancers'll come.'

'And when the party's over.'

'Find another sky.'

People Out Walking
and Pointing

On the damp side of the road where there are lilies, onion flowers, sweet peas, wild turnips and all sorts of seeding grasses, there were two women walking. They both had white hair and wore dresses that needed no ironing, dresses that could be washed, put on a hanger and allowed to drip dry. After only an hour or two the dresses could be brought in ready to wear. Both dresses were open at the neck, had collars and lapels, and were buttoned to the waist. One was hooped all the way down with differing widths of white and pale turquoise stripes, the other was navy, patterned with red triangles which intersected in groups of threes. Skirts were permanently pleated. The women wore stockings, and shoes that were not quite sandals but had cutout toes and heels. Beige, biscuit, bone, off-white, ivory, cream, almond — or whatever that colour is called this year.

The women stopped every now and again along the way to point at the grasses and other plants beside the footpath. They would've been naming the plants, reminding each other of names, as though to name, to remember, was a possession greater than holding in the hand, ownership more permanent than pleating. Forever, as long as fabric didn't wear thin.

But they would've been remembering more than names. They'd have been taking hold of times when grasses told you who you would marry, of times when they'd spent hours collecting seeds of rye in a tobacco tin for the war effort. There were stalks of soldiers in their brown uniforms and yellow-brimmed hats that could be picked, and with a flick an enemy soldier's head could be snapped clean off. There were grasses that could be unsheathed to make darts and spears, and heads of grass than when tucked inside a sleeve would make their way up your arm to your chest. Stab you in the heart if left long enough. Kill you.

At the bend, on the sea side of the road, there is a wide footpath and a culverted stone wall. There are wooden ramps and concrete steps leading down to the sand. Standing on the edge of the wall were two boys looking down. One was bending, hands on knees, looking, looking. The other was showing him, not just pointing, but bringing his arm right back until his elbow made a sharp triangle behind his shoulder and his stretched finger lay parallel to his ear. Then his whole arm thrust forward, See, like a boxer giving out a succession of straight-arm punches, See, See, See, as if the more energy he put into the indications the quicker his friend would discover what it was he was being shown.

But he, the one seeing and pointing — at a dollar coin, or a special stone or shell — wouldn't jump and get it ahead of his friend because he wanted to fight him for it, beat him to it on equal terms.

At last the friend saw, and the boys jumped off the wall together, grabbing at each other as they fell.

There's a rocky outcrop at the end of the first bay where the sea wall tapers down. Two men had walked out onto the rocks and were looking down into the pools at nothing extraordinary. They were conversing, pointing here and there, perhaps at colours, shapes, anemone, weed, sedimentation. Neither was dressed for the beach or rock walking. They wore buttoned shirts, light trousers and slip-on shoes. One had a parcel under his arm.

Out on the sea, beyond the rocks, were two people in a canoe making a turn to go into the next bay. On the beach by the water's edge a man and a woman were trying to show a child that the canoe was coming. See, see, there, don't look at my finger look where I'm pointing. But the child was too small and struggled in her father's arms, leaning down, wanting to play in the water.

This all happened while I was driving along the beach road on my way to the craft fair. Winter had been long and harsh, spring wet and cool. People were pleased to be out.

I had difficulty finding a place to park when I reached the town centre because it was the day of the Santa Parade. Lyttelton Avenue and Parumoana Street had been blocked off to traffic and hundreds of people were lining the roads waiting.

There was music coming from somewhere. Food carts, tents and stalls for the fair had been set up all over Te Rauparaha Park, where in 1979 there had been an immolation.

Boiling

Macky wondered what Charlotte would do about Lizzie's boils. He didn't care much. The sun was a big boil in the sky. He could hear Denny Boy coming, racketing with a stick along Aunty Myra's corrugated fence.

Denny Boy pulled a wire scramble out of his pocket. 'All by hand,' he said.

Macky looked hard at the wire that had been twisted, looped and tied into a tangle, looking for signs that it could have had pliers or a hammer used on it, or that it could have been pounded with a stone. He decided that it had been done by hand as Denny Boy said. 'How long I got?' he asked.

'Count to a hundred.'

'For what?'

'Gooseberries from Aunty Myra's.'

Macky wasn't impressed with that. He knew he could pinch Aunty Myra's goosegogs any time. 'Give it to Charlotte,' he said.

Charlotte was sitting on the doorstep. She was in a trance.

'Wanna go?' Denny Boy called, holding up the tangle.

She ignored him and went inside.

In the bedroom Mereana was sitting at the end of the bed looking goofy, while Lizzie was lying on her stomach being unable to move for boils on her backside which had spread down her legs to the backs of her knees. 'Aaa, aaa,' Lizzie was saying from deep inside her.

She knew, and they all knew, that the boils had been given to her by a witch on the day she'd run last down Witch Woman's path, coughing.

The night before, Aunty Connie had bathed the boils with hot water and packed them in a bread poultice, but nothing had happened. Now Aunty had gone next door after telling the kids to help Lizzie down to the sea. So Charlotte and Macky, with Mereana following, had shouldered under Lizzie's armpits and taken her out up to her neck in the water and stayed there until the tide went down. Nothing happened except that Lizzie whitened and went soft, and the boils that had been red and plummy became motley and pale like birds' eggs.

But on their way back up the beach to the house Charlotte had made a promise. 'I'll fix them,' she'd said.

It was on the way home on the last day of school for the year that the kids had decided they'd find out for once and for all if it was true that Witch Woman had killed her husband and buried him in the basement along with a string of babies.

Aunty Connie, when they'd asked her, had said no. She'd said that Witch Woman was just someone ordinary who'd gone a bit funny and who never had a husband in the first place. 'Nearly but he got away,' she'd said, not addressing them at all, but talking instead, over the tops of their heads, to Uncle Jack and Aunty Myra.

Well, the kids knew not to expect too much of adults. They knew that grown-ups made jokes out of everything, kept half-secrets, told lies just to make other adults, who already knew the truth or lies, laugh. They also knew that when adults, uncles especially, decided to talk straight to your face they wouldn't lie for anything, even though the truth they told at those times was still only to make other adults laugh — nose like your mother, feet like your father and black as a pot.

'Remember her sitting up on the gate when me and Kepa

was breaking in Rigger,' Uncle Jack had said, 'giving us a bit of a poppy show? Kep reckoned we should get the bit between the teeth there too, get the bridle on, but all talk, we done nothing.' That was in the days when Uncle Jack had juices up to his eyeballs, which nowadays had all sunk to his feet.

'Knock on the door, talk to her,' Charlotte said to Mereana and Lizzie. 'Us'll go and look in the basement window see any graves.'

Mereana and Lizzie didn't want to be the ones to go to the door, and even though they knew that Charlotte would probably prove too strong for them in the end, there was still a way to go before they reached Witch Woman's house, time yet to think of some way out of it as they walked along the sand and up along the top of the sea wall. They started saying what if.

'What if she pull us inside?'

'Knock and stand back,' said Charlotte.

'What if she chase us?'

'She can't catch you.'

'What if she turn us into spiders?' Mereana and Lizzie knew they were risking scorn by asking such a question but they were buying time. Also they wanted to know what Charlotte *really* believed.

'She's too weak for that,' said Charlotte who knew everything.

And what Charlotte said seemed to be true. Witch Woman was little and papery with a torn scrap face, a crumple of lemony hair and watery eyes that looked as if they'd been pressed into her head by a pair of dirty thumbs. She walked down the road sometimes, in sandshoes and raincoat, carrying a string bag that was like an old fungus, and never looked at you even if you called out to her. She never shopped, ate or had cat companions. Her arms hung by her sides like doll arms.

'And anyway she's a *real* witch,' Charlotte said, knowing everything. 'Not just one out of a story flying on brooms.'

Macky and Denny Boy nodded their heads as though they too knew all the things that Charlotte knew, but Lizzie and Mereana knew they'd never even thought of it.

The sea wall ended, giving way to a rocky shore between one bay and the next, and as the children made their way up to the road that went round the hill to Witch Woman's house Lizzie made one last attempt to get them out of it. 'We scared,' she said.

But it was a mistake. Charlotte had been expecting this and now she paused, held her breath a moment, then whispered as if out of admiration, 'You jumped.' And as soon as she said it both Lizzie and Mereana knew what they'd known all along, that Charlotte was too strong for them and that they would have to be the ones to go knocking.

'You jumped.' No triumph in her voice. 'You jumped,' said just the right way — Lizzie not able to deny she'd jumped, Mereana not able to say, 'Wasn't me, only her, jumped,' as if she would now leave Lizzie alone to knock on the Witch's door.

From beside the pool Mereana had watched Lizzie on Big Rock, standing as still as the rock itself, toes gripping the ledge. Would she jump? Mereana knew she would. All of them watching from the pool's edge, the rock ledges, the banks, knew. Willed her.

To jump.

Not to jump.

Everything in the whole world quiet. No word that would make any of them to blame if she did. No word to stop her.

Would she?

If she did would she die? Mereana's heart was Lizzie's heart. Her stomach was Lizzie's stomach.

She saw Lizzie's legs skip and kick, then Lizzie was out in

flickering space, no more than a weighted shimmer, dropping, all of them to blame. The dark pool face split open, then closed and the whole world was soundless and upside down.

Waiting.

Not knowing if Lizzie was big enough, heavy enough to touch bottom and push off, shoot for the surface, find it.

Waiting, the valley booming its stillness; the dark trees, the rocks, the banks leaning; the sky drumming down.

Until the upside-down broke, casting Lizzie's face up from it — a face daubed and fish-looking, piping thin air. There was a leaning back then, a retreating of sky. Charlotte and Denny Boy were up and swearing because they were older than anyone else and would have been to blame.

'You jumped,' said Charlotte.

That was it. The two girls turned towards the dirt path that led to Witch Woman's house, pushing past a wattle tree that rattled tan fingers of seed pods as they made their way through and past flax bushes and an overgrowth of fat-leaved hedge that was poison smelling.

By the door they stood on a patch of yard by a tealeaf pile. There was a birdy, old-straw smell. Chooky, even though there were no hens about. And combined with this was a thick smell of black water with grey bubbles on it where clothes have been soaking two days, that has been flung out over a yard with the sun beating down.

The girls stood for a moment, Lizzie hunching and wriggling her knitting-needle frame about inside her dress, which was sleeveless and loose, and seemed as she moved about, not to be touched by any part of her. Mereana stood beside her, filling out the same cut of dress with no room to move about inside it at all. They fixed their eyes on the face of the sunburnt door, then stepped forward together, knocked and stood back.

There was a scrabbling from behind the door as of someone coming to them through paper, and eventually the door opened and Witch Woman was there, not looking at them, but looking instead at the chooky ground, shivering as though it could be a cold day.

'Good afternoon,' the girls said together, and they thought the woman's whitebaity lips moved but they weren't sure.

'We come,' said Lizzie; but couldn't remember what Charlotte had told them to say and only giggles came out of her. The giggles made her cough.

'And,' said Mereana, 'and . . .' The woman who buried babies stood trembling as though she could be cold.

It was while Lizzie was busy with her coughing, and while they were both trying to remember what Charlotte had told them to say, that Mereana heard the others yelling and scrambling, then beating it along the road.

So she bolted, leaving Lizzie to choke along behind her down the path, past the flax, the poison, the rattle hands, down to the road where the others were dust.

'Tell,' she called, running but with no hope of catching up.

'Tell,' Lizzie squealed behind her.

'Tell.'

'Tell.'

Without slowing down or turning, the voices of the others came rocking back over their heads, back through the turning road dust and the shadow that the hill made.

'Spayaydes.'

'Spay.'

'Spaydes.'

'Got shovels.'

'Shovels and.'

'And spa-a-a-des.'

Charlotte, doing her best to keep the trance, looked about the room for clues as to what she could do about the boils. There was a bed, a window with a cube of sun coming in, the buckled ceiling held by its cross-pieces. There was a wardrobe with a diamond-shaped mirror on the door, an old calendar with a picture of kittens on it that had a threaded needle and some pins stuck in round its edges. There was the lightbulb wearing a yellowy shade with a bite out of it. There was the light-string with a plait of wool that Aunty Connie had joined onto it, making it long enough to feed through a hook at the top of the bed where it was hitched by a red button. On the wall above the bed was a blanched kewpie doll on a stick that Aunty June who had died had won at a fair some years before. The doll wore two layers of limp net edged in peeled silver round her middle, and a sprinkle of glitter on her head which was stuck there with a crust of brown glue. On the hook of the stick was a bunch of balding feathers. 'We use that,' Charlotte said.

She went to the wardrobe and took out two floral scarves and a dark blue chiffon dressing gown that Uncle Kepa had brought home from another country. Charlotte gave these to Mereana to hold then went out to the kitchen where she stoked up the stove, fed some wood in and shifted the kerosene tin of water across.

Then she went down to the beach, keeping her trance past Macky and Denny Boy, and waded out to the post where Uncle Kepa kept crayfish in a cage. There were several crayfish in there and she took two. 'What for?' Macky called, but she didn't answer. She saw that he'd been undoing the wire tangle that Denny Boy made — huh, just for goosegogs. As she went by with the crayfish the boys stood and followed her.

Charlotte put the crayfish on the bench telling Macky and Denny Boy not to let them crawl off, and to bring the tin and the crayfish once the water boiled.

In the bedroom Charlotte put the chiffon gown on over her clothes, rolled the sleeves of it up to her shoulders and told Mereana to fasten them there with pins from the calendar. She tied one of the scarves round Mereana's waist, one round her shoulders and gave her the kewpie doll to hold.

When the water was ready Macky and Denny Boy brought the tin into the bedroom, put it down on the floor and fetched the crayfish. Charlotte stood the boys in the door frame, and when everything was ready, told Mereana to touch Lizzie's forehead with the kewpie doll and to hold it there.

Charlotte, with a crayfish in each hand, knelt by the tin and let her face sit in the steam while she perfected her trance. Then she stretched her arms upwards, lifting the crayfish that waved their legs at the criss-crossed ceiling as though they might walk there. She threw her head back and shouted at the boils to go away forever. 'Go for once and forever.' Then she plunged the crayfish and her arms into the water.

At the sight of this Lizzie screamed, jumped up on the bed and cracked herself against the wall as though trying to escape through it.

Then the boils broke, pus and blood began streaming and the cores popped like peas.

Mereana, Macky and Denny Boy watched all of this happen while Charlotte ran, yelling, in the gown from another country, to sit herself in the sea.

Old Ones Become Birds

She thought of bedsocks like the ones she'd seen at the Martinborough Fair, knitted in double bluegreen — stockingstitch in the foot, patterned above, with crocheted drawstrings threaded round the ankles. Same pattern as baby booties, only large. Had thought of buying a pair but it was summer then.

The light near the door was on but the rest of the house was dark and beginning to snore. Woman on the mattress on one side of her was tuning up, and on the other side was an old wheezer. Oldies all having early nights. She settled into the sleeping bag trying not to rustle. Rugby socks would've done the trick.

Anyway she was pleased to have found a space in the main sleeping house, knowing that out in the 'barracks' the young ones would be up talking half the night — preparing workshops or just fooling about. Even now she could hear them coming and going, singing, laughing. But only sounds. Far enough away to be soothing as she lay rubbing blood down into her feet. In the morning some of them would be out doing aerobics with Gus. In the morning there'd be ice.

The birds started up, but that was later. Before that, before light, in the deep morning, the tuner next to her began rattling her baggage and murmuring to her companion on the far side. The two put on coats and began making their way, feeling each footstep, chatting loud enough for their own old ears about a torch that one of them had and who it belonged to originally and who that person's father and mother were, and who the grandparents were and where they were originally from. The door opened. No light to come in through it but soon there was torchlight jigging away in the direction of the washroom.

By the time the two returned the coughing had started, the talk, the movement to sit up and wait for light, the to-ing and fro-ing in the dark to the showers, whizzing of atomisers. The women made their way in and got back in under their quilts to wait. The shower was good and hot it seemed.

On the other side of her the old wheezer was pulling on socks, putting a coat over his pyjamas and she expected he was going for a shower too. But no, he was making his way to a space between the window and door, tapping the pou and beginning to chant the morning karakia. Around the house others were joining in, picking up for him when his breath ran out, these first birds.

She knew they wouldn't be let off lightly with the invocations, which seemed timeless and unending and so early, old bird. Restful once she'd accepted that there'd be no more sleep for her that morning. She closed her eyes and let the singsong wash, and when she opened them again dawn had been canted in. She lay and waited for full light.

Hard frost, and a few out with Gus doing aerobics guitar-style. Then a cold shower that she was not keen enough to get right under, but she washed and put on most of the clothing she'd brought with her. Back out in the white she found two mates to walk with before breakfast, comparing nights and the state of showers.

They walked in a white world, along white tracks, through white paddocks, by white fenceposts wired silver. Cobwebs in filigree. Glass trees. Her words were carried on white breath telling of the early-early birds, and back on white breath came the telling about the night in the barracks that had been noisy and cold. One of her companions had managed to sleep through it, one hadn't. Sky of steel with sun burning a white hole in it.

Seating had been arranged in front of the meeting house and the old ones had already found their places. They were animated, chirpy, turning their faces to the sun as they waited for the unveiling of the carved stone which was the first event on the programme for the day. Once the words had been said and the kakahu removed the olds led them all by the carved piece so they could all see and touch it. She watched them ahead of her as they clutched about them their coloured shawls and rugs, fluffing them featherly, beaking the ground with their sticks, eyeing from side to side, feet big and spread in hugboots, ugboots, gumboots and shoes.

At the main meeting of the day the elders had a great deal to say on the subject of oral histories. Stories, if that's what it meant. Life, if that's what it meant. Yeh, yeh, they don't mind telling the stories, long as the stories don't get stolen so all those Pakehas go and make money. And don't want their stories thieved by all those archive people too. It's for our own. That's that. Our own mokopuna. Don't want our own people ripping us off too, it's for the kids.

By afternoon the heads were dropping wingward, the birdlids beginning to droop over bird eyes. Up to everybody else those other things — recommendations, delegations, applications, justifications. Had enough of that but we support the idea, the recording of stories so the children will know. Otherwise, if we didn't support it wouldn't be here with a rumatiki and a flu, middle of winter, telling it.

After a while she realised many of the seats were empty.

There'd been a quiet exit of olds. In on the mattresses for an hour or two before mealtime she guessed.

Or gone flying.

She looked up. Yes, there they all were in their bird colours. Become birds.

There, beating up into the sky that deepened as their many-coloured wings blocked the sun, while from their throats came the chatter, taptap, call, chant, scratch, wheeze.

It wasn't long before she felt herself rising.

My Leanne

I found a seat by the window where I could sit and see my Leanne. I could look out and we could lock our eyes together as the doors slapped shut and the bus shuffled off. My Leanne. Waiting by the bus shelter which has been painted by Intermediate kids during a city awareness project. Bright colours — tapa patterns, ponga trees, fern fronds and hibiscus, which says heaps about our city I suppose.

Black eyes, large teeth and the way she smiles, laughs, plaits her hair in a thick sausage and loops it up to sit at the back of her neck — the way she walks, the fun she has. I fell in love with her a year ago on Monster Raffle Day.

Schools organise these days to raise funds. It's some rip-off deal with a company where schools get a share of the profits for doing all the selling. Teachers arrange the school side of it, gridding the selling places, assigning the areas and coaching up the kids. You can get out of it on religious grounds or by flatly refusing, but then teachers'll go on about school spirit, sharing responsibilities, and remind us that those that don't take part will have written assignments to do on the day. There's always a half day off school for the class that sells the most tickets.

I was happy to go out and sell tickets when I found my selling partner was to be Leanne.

I'm all right. Not ugly, vice-captain of the second fifteen, been in the school band for two years, popular enough. Nobody says, what's Leanne doing going out with a jerk like that?

We had a good patch by McDonald's, a pharmacy and three

banks — Leanne, me and a couple of third formers. It was a
Thursday, chosen because it was the day when all the old age
people, the DPBs and UPBs collected their benefits. Lots of
people about. We sold heaps and I believed it was that smile of
Leanne's that roped people in. At the end of the day, after the
vans had done the rounds and collected our ticket boards and
money bags I asked her to come to the movies with me. But she
told me, not in any embarrassed way, that her parents wouldn't
let her go out at night with friends. I was disappointed but felt
that she liked me and that she was pleased I'd asked her.

At school the next day I went to the notice board and found
out where her team was playing, and on Saturday turned up to
her game. That afternoon she came to rugby with me and we
walked home together afterwards.

From then on we began to spend more and more time
together, walking together to and from school, sitting together
at lunch breaks and attending each other's games. I began to
resent it if friends decided to walk along with us or if they sat
with us at lunchtime. After a while they left us alone.

There are some things you do that you don't want to do. It's
the last thing you want. It's like when you shoot a bird with a
slug gun. You didn't want the bird to be dead but you wanted to
shoot it. Had to. You didn't want to shoot a tin off a rock, a light
off a lamp-post, a shed window because you'd done enough of
that. It had to be a bird. You had to see it jerk up out of a tree
squawking, drop on the path and lie there twitching. Then you
had to do it again.

Sundays were the only days that I didn't see Leanne. She
had church in the mornings, church in the evenings and church
in between.

At first I didn't mind. I'd just go off and watch the softball,
or sometimes have a game of touch. Then I started to think how
Sunday was the only day, with no school, no organised sports,

that Leanne and I could've been really alone, different from sitting by ourselves in school classrooms or walking the streets to and from school or watching each other from sidelines. Why would she want to go to church all day instead of being with me, was what I kept thinking.

So I asked her one Monday morning, making it sound as joking as I could.

'There's no choice in our family,' she said.

'So you say,' I said, 'but there must be something to interest you there.'

She looked at me in a questioning way.

There's something in me, something that isn't part of my intelligence, something that started off small then began to grow. It seems to have started from love.

I began to question Leanne more and more about what went on at church, what was so good about church, who was so interesting at church. At first she'd answer me in her own smiling way, not quite joking, not quite serious. Until her smile made me mad.

And other times I wanted to know who she sat next to in class and what was so good about so-and-so. What was the big deal about leaping round all over the netball courts with everybody gawking. I could hear myself but couldn't quite believe what I heard. All I really wanted to do was hold her, kiss her, get down with her, love her.

She said her parents would kill her if we did, said she wasn't ready for that and anyway wouldn't want to in bushes or parks or some mate's place at lunchtime.

Excuses, there was someone she was having it with at church. I'd heard of churches like that.

'Don't . . .'

'Don't.' Mimicking, listening to myself.

After school Leanne would walk with me to the bus stop

where I'd catch the bus to my afternoon job and I'd get a window seat where I could look out until the bus left.

It was just as the bus pulled out that afternoon that I saw Rexie Thomas come up and stand beside her. He's a scumball slob with a fat guts and a moony face, famous for taking a farting cushion into the exam room and letting off loud noises. He looks like a huge baby except babies aren't so loony looking. He always wears the worst option of our school uniform which is grey shorts, grey shirt, blue jersey and sandals. Doesn't matter if it's summer or winter, it's sandals and jersey for Rexie. I got out of my seat and went to the back of the bus and saw Leanne going off with him.

I didn't see Leanne the next morning because her form class was going out on a research trip and they were all meeting at the railway station. For once I didn't mind. I'd been doing some thinking. I really did want Leanne, didn't want to drive her away and knew I had to get my head round this. So I thought about love and happiness and how if you love someone you must want them to be happy. It seemed simple.

But then I had to think that if you made someone unhappy, miserable, got enjoyment out of seeing her smile disappear then you didn't love her at all. There was something missing from these equations but I couldn't figure out what it was.

Anyway I made some resolutions, thought about words to say. I felt all right as I went to the place where we'd arranged to meet that afternoon.

She was late. Leanne was always on time but today she was late. She was late or not coming, late or not coming. Late. Not coming. Late. Not coming, not coming.

But then she came, hurrying, smiling, beautiful.

'Dean, it took longer than we expected. We missed the twenty-to and had to get the twenty-past.'

'What about him?' I said.

'Who?'

'Fartface Rexie.'

'Rexie. Yes, he was there.'

'So I suppose you've arranged to meet him again, like you did yesterday?'

'I didn't arrange anything yesterday.'

'I saw you, remember? At the bus stop?'

'That wasn't arranged. He was just coming along.'

'Yeah yeah.'

'It's true. He waited so we could walk home together. He lives next door, you know that. He's always lived next door. Our two families have always known each other. All of us kids have grown up together. We all go to the same church. Rexie and I were born in the same month, we went to the same play group, started primary school on the same day. We've been in the same class all the way through primary. We're in the same class again.'

I knew that everything she was saying was true. I know where Leanne lives, where Rexie lives, where they all went to primary — which is only two streets away from where I went to primary myself. I know all of Rexie's family and all of Leanne's family. I knew Leanne wasn't in love with Rexie. I knew it was true that she hadn't arranged to meet him.

I said, 'If there's all that between you you should go and have a fuck with him then.'

She turned and stepped out and a van knocked her to the other side of the street where she was hit by two cars.

The sound of it is something I can't forget, can't forget what she looked like.

She wasn't dead. The ambulance came. Someone took me home.

I stopped going to school. I suppose teachers and classmates thought I was in at the hospital seeing Leanne, but I couldn't face going to see her, even though I believe she asked for me once

she began to recover. I didn't want to go anywhere, or see anyone.
Didn't want anyone to see me. I'd get up and get ready for school
so that my mother wouldn't pester me, then when she'd gone to
work I'd go and lie down on my bed, or sometimes sit on the
edge of it, leaning with my fingers locked together, and it was as
though I couldn't move. Sometimes there was someone else in
the room with me, someone shadowy, but bloated and bruised
and groaning. Whoever it was wanted to kill me.

One Sunday Rexie rang my mother and asked her to tell me
he was coming to pick me up to take me to visit Leanne. Mum
got clothes ready for me and something to take in a tin. Pestered
me. Then she and Dad went off with the kids to watch Deb's
game.

So I dressed, and while I was waiting for Rexie I went to the
kitchen for a knife because I wanted to cut away the awful things,
the bad things inside, the wrong parts. There's a butcher knife
that's worn and fine. Had to.

Knife in my hand. In my hand the handle of it warming.
Hand hesitating. Hand not knowing. Hand not knowing where
to begin. Heart could be right. Heart could be the right place to
begin.

Chocolate Cake Raffle

On the morning that I woke up not thinking first of Clark I decided to go door-to-door with a chocolate cake raffle. It was a warm day. Warm wind starting up.

I spread two pieces of toast with honey and heaped slices of tamarillo and cheese onto them. Put them under the grill. Scoffed. Then drank two slow cups of coffee. Snootily. Like saying, stuff you, Clark.

After I'd taken a long time over coffee I numbered down in an old notebook and wrote on the inside of the cover: 'Chocolate Cake Raffle in aid of carved gateway. Tickets $1.'

Just as I finished my mother came in from the bedroom, my father came in from outside and they both stared at my plates and cup, my clothes, the notebook and pen — not talking, not talking, not talking. Then my mother said, 'What're you doing today?'

'Fund-raising,' I said.

'A raffle or something?'

'Chocolate cake.'

'You know, that gateway,' she said, 'they're making it too flash. Don't have to be that big and flash and cost so much. A carved pou each side, painted arch would be all right. Neat and tidy. No, they have to go for back and front carvings, up down and sideways, all those tongues poking in all directions as if money comes down with rain. How much a ticket?'

'A dollar.' My parents were looking over my head as they scratched for their dollars, splashing their eyes at each other.

Getting back to normal, getting over it, said their splashing-at-each-other eyes.

Off I went.

For one whole Saturday, I watched from my window a girl going from house to house with a chocolate cake raffle, hair done up high, spouting out of its cerise band and rippling down like a black fountain. Bike shorts and a ming top with black wild-hair figures dancing and drumming all over. Sleeveless, with a stand-up collar. Big, hunky sports shoes without socks, cut low enough at the backs to show bony ankles and deep hollows above the heels. What else? Muscly legs, skin smooth and dark brown. Face triangular — that is, pointed chin, cheekbones like doorknobs under squeezed eyes. It's as if her face could've been pulled upwards by the too-tight topknot, if I hadn't known different. Good-sized nose in the middle of it and good teeth crossing each other. Bangles, or is bracelets the word to use? And large paua shell star on a chain round her neck, moons on her ears. Notebook in a plastic bag is what she carried.

Girl? I know it's not good these days, calling someone grown a 'girl'. 'Woman' or 'young woman' is right. But jangle, thin and smartstep is 'girl' to me, smell of feijoas is 'girl' to me from my high window, from my eye warts and white hair age. 'Girl' is all I can say.

My cousin, knitting slippers, stopped that and showed me where the old back porch had been pulled down and the kitchen extended. New plumbing, everything formica, new paint and new backdoor with glass of tulips.

'So where is it?' he asked as he took up the knitting again.

'Not made yet. Tonight, or tomorrow, after all the tickets are sold I'll make it.'

'Your mum's usual chockie cake recipe?'

'Doubled. Cooked in the biggest tin.'

'Round or square?'

'Round.'

'Chocolate icing?'

'Mm, and walnuts, or coconut.'

'Not coconut. Coconut is mean looking, or looks as if you're covering up messes or mistakes, or as if the icing didn't set properly.'

'All right, walnuts.'

'And no hundreds and thousands. They leak, ooze their colours, and they're kiddie-looking.'

'No, I wasn't thinking of hundreds and thousands. Just walnuts then, proper halves.'

He leafed through the notebook studying numbers, telling me he'd have to stop all this knitting and get outside on a day like this. Trouble was he had orders from this one and that one who were all getting on his back about it. It was making him fat, sitting round knitting.

'Who?'

'All the old ducks. They want knitted slippers to wear in the meeting houses when they go away tipi haere all over the place. It's the in thing. Trouble is they give them away to mates then they want some more.'

'Tell them to make their own. Give them the recipe. Take the pattern down to the training scheme building and photocopy it.'

'They've got arthritis and emphysema and they haven't got time, they reckon. One excuse or another.'

'I might give you a hand if you show me.'

'You need size three-and-a-quarter and fives, or I might have spare pairs.'

'I'll look through Mum's, or get some.'

'Okay. All right. Tonight or tomorrow, when I win, when you

bring my cake I'll show you. And you can tell me all the news then, about Whatshisface.'

'Him?'

'Mm.'

'Hmm.'

Anyway why do I need to use any of those words — 'girl', 'woman', 'young woman' — when I've known her name since the day it was given to her — Donita Marisse. Awg. But she's known as Nita. No teeth till a year old. No hair. Fat, gummy chuckler.

More than a year ago she brought this Partner to meet me. Not Boyfriend, Husband, Friend or Fiancé, but Partner. As if the two of them might've been a well-known pair, or in business together like Dean and Jerry, Makepeace and Cooch, Whitcombe and Tombs, Simon and Garfunkle, Topp Twins, Batman and Robin.

But of course I knew what she meant. He had black, bristly hair and dark eyes. He was handsome and tallowy, trim, match fit — like a policeman or a young Mormon — and she wore him like a trophy. It was as if she'd gone to Barcelona and come back with gold after false starts, disasters and unpromising beginnings. Now at last she'd done it. Together they looked kind of legendary and sculptured.

But it's all over. She's been home a week shut away in her room. Not talking to anyone, her mother said. Until now. Now she's out high-stepping with a raffle. Chocolate cake I'm guessing. Keni'll be getting the lowdown on the breakup of the partnership, or maybe not. They could be talking home alterations instead. He promised he'd have the slippers finished before tomorrow when I leave for Morrinsville early hours of the morning. They're woolmix — green and orange. Nice. I hope no one asks me for them. If I win the cake she can give it to Keni for making me the slippers. He's little and coppery, green-eyed and growing a paunch.

The Johnsons were loading stuff to take to the tip. They had hangovers from their work party. Ned and Judy. Olly was looking out of the window. Two of the kids were in the car waiting to go, and a third, the eldest, was on the trampoline bouncing.

'When we going, when we going?' called the kids from the car.

'Keep quiet, stop calling,' their parents said. 'Say hello to Nita.'

'Cake raffle, in aid of the gateway. Chocolate cake with chocolate icing and walnuts.'

'Don't mention it. It don't sound very nice at this moment.'

'Go in and get some money off Olly.'

'Come in,' said Olly out the window.

'What about whipped cream?' said Olly.

'I thought of it,' I said. 'But it gets messy when you try to cut it.'

'Sharp knife,' Olly said. 'Long and thin. You pop the knife in, keep it upright while you jig it up and down. Don't bring the knife down across it.'

'I could then, have cream, slice it through the middle, whip some up, fill it. I don't know if cream goes with walnuts.'

'Cherries and strawberries. Or grapes maybe. Might have to be grapes, not likely to be cherries and strawbs this time of the year.'

Hinewai is on the trampoline. All I see from here is a head and half torso bobbing up above the shed wall, her hair sleeking down as she rises, streaming up as she drops. It's like when the tides wash and backwash seaweed between the rocks. Up on the hill behind them the trees are swinging in the wind that's come up, leaves showing their undersides. All the mixed greens. All the rolling green heads.

The rubbish Ned and Judy are piling is mainly fennel that they've been cutting at the back of their uncle's house next door. He's my brother.

Fennel, stinkweed, hemlock, devil's grass. If you go out to dinner to some swanky place you're likely to get a little feather of it on your plate poisoning your fish. We broke off dry stalks of it when we were kids, lit it and smoked it. Once we set the orchard on fire with a dropped match and watched the flame run, divide itself, fly along like a flock of red birds through the dry grass.

The people came with wet bags, driving the red birds to the creek where they all drowned. We were hiding, watching from the hill.

'Get a goat,' I said to Ned, Judy and Olly when they were hacking at the fennel, which every half year they do. 'Or build you a house there,' I said to Olly.

'One day,' she said.

I saw Nita speak through the window and go inside. After a while she came out and went next door to my brother's.

'Now Myrtle in Auckland with her cafe does one this size,' said Pop Hepa into the circle of his arms. 'Choc Attack it's called.' But he pronounced Choc like Shock. 'Icing, cream, grapes, peaches, mandareens, cherries. Strawberries covered in shocolate, in three layers. Jam I think too. That's her. Myrtle in Auckland. Three dollars fifty a slice and not a bit left every day. I don't know. I'm not a hundred per cent certain about the jam. If she runs out of time the oldest one does it. Awhina. Cooks it and decorates it all herself. Only thirteen. Bright. Showed us all her school reports, doing all right. Mm. Myrtle and Gordon in Auckland doing okay for themselves.

'We come back from Auckland and next thing your aunty wants to go down south to Mita and Ken. But I like my own bed, my own cooking, my own TAB, my own time. I told her to go on her own and that's where she is . . . Well, what's here?' he said into his pocket. 'A two and a one. Okay give me three. Find me numbers with sevens and fours. Yes, Myrtle. It was my birthday, seventy-four while we're up there. I told them I don't want a birthday, leave me. No, they had to. Presents, cards, drinks, dinner, shock attack, candles, the lot. Photos, I'll show you.'

He put his washing out early — a towel, socks, underpants, singlet, two shirts, all flapping on a line strung between the puriri tree and a pole from the old revolving line. They never liked the revolving one, Hepa and Hazel. They prefer the strung-out one and a real good flap.

Two kereru have been coming these past two seasons, when the berries are ripe, to the puriri tree. Coming in, departing, right by my window.

My ears found it hard to believe what they heard the first time, after so many years. The noisy whistling kereru wingbeats were sounds only heard in thick bush when I was young. Now they have come to feed in gardens. I hurried to the window, then I saw them. It was as if they had come from a time, rather than a place as I looked down from the high window on polished green plumage, rouged backs and wings, almost into the garnet eyes. I opened my window and called a greeting to the dark tails, wanting to shout, 'Who are you? Who are you?' but it's not polite.

He'll be telling about Auckland, about daughter, son-in-law and grandkids. They got him to go up there after all these years and he had the time of his life. But he wouldn't go south to the other one, Haze had to go on her own. He'll be bringing out the photos taken at his birthday party.

The driveway up the hill has been concreted since I was here last. Cousins are tuning up. No dust now, no mud. Two humps to slow the vehicles, but nothing slows the kids on bikes who zig round the outsides of the humps calling, 'Hi Nita!' to me.

The car has been shifted out and my cousins have set up the gears in the garage. 'Come for a jam?' they asked.

'Come on, give us some vocals.'

'Where's that movie star you been towing, do a runner?'

'Trade him in?'

'Sleazeball I bet. Looked a bit of a sleazeball to me.'

I took the mike. 'I don't wanna talk about it,' I sang into it, 'how you broke my heart.' Jason and Hones picking and bassing along after me on the guitars. 'If I stay here just a little bit longer Oo ee-oo, Won't you listen, to my hea-a-a-art?' Ladygirl plenty of rumbles and trembles, slap-slap, swish-swish and wish-wash on the percussions, 'Whoa-aa-aa stars in the sky don't mean nothin' to you, they're a mirror,' and all that.

After a while we jazzed up for a time, bluesed down, then forwardsed our way through to, 'Evrythin gonna be all right, waa-a-aa.'

Woo-oo-oo the wind up clattering its beat through the gaps. Till dark.

That's her, Nita, singing. She's the youngest of six, born when her brothers and sisters were already grown. Born singing. Dumpling singer, spoiled and put on show. She knew all the songs of the day as well as all the oldtimers. TV ads and theme songs too, start to finish without missing a word or a beat. She could lead, take parts, back up, fill all the gaps, all by the time she was seven.

And oh listen. It's a follow-me follow-me surprise of singing as always, that takes you by the throat and you dangle, you dangle, she dangles you. There you are reaching, wanting to stay with her but all the time she's beyond and you're scrambling. Sometimes for a line or two she'll pick you up and take you with her. There you are so grateful, cupped and drifting, then suddenly you're on a point, spinning, then reaching and scrambling again.

Longing.

And when you're put down at last you know you're someone different from who you were before. Some aching thing has been either added to or taken away from who you are or were. Added or taken, it's difficult to tell which. It's as if there's an iridescent bead that's found it's way in under the ribs, or perhaps rolled, without noise, away from there.

Which doesn't at all mean that life will end in tragedy.

But listen. It's why all the windows are open. Why mine is. It's why Hepa is out under his tree.

It's why Keni's out on his steps with his needles and wool ball. It's why Ned and Judy are out piling yet another load and why Olly has come out to help. It's why Hinewai, Tama and Maureen are lying flat on the trampoline. Why Mere, Terry and Duane are smooth-riding, patterning the tracks on their bikes, single file, twos, threes, gliding like porpoises, leaping the humps together, riding in song. She's here, she's home is what the songs tell us. Evrythin gonna be all right.

For now.

While the sky changes colour and the hills deepen, while the very last note is held, held — Jason, Hones and Ladygirl following tamping, tamping, fingering, picking along until they all, together, bring it down.

Gone.

In week or two she'll be gone.

I see her coming as kids are called in, as parents leave their piling, as Keni jabs needles into the ball, as my brother leaves his pigeon tree, as we draw back from our windows.

Coming to tell.

Under the purple dark, coming with her notebook to knock on my door.

Harp Music

There is a girl. She was playing a harp. I forgot about her for fifty years but when I saw her again I remembered how I liked her. Loved her.

Because of my resolution to scale down, to stop being everything to everyone and to prioritise time, I wasn't enthusiastic about going to the school gala. I'd intended giving Jemma twenty bucks as my contribution so that I could stay home and get on with the work. I would have a warm room, my tapes and books, my neat notes and I would begin this weekend.

But the grandkids rang me about the gala. 'We're in the orchestra,' they said. 'And the kapa haka.'

'I'll bring your cousins,' I said. 'Lana, Tana and Banana,' (to crack them up). 'Aunty Jem's coming with Tiria. Your uncles'll come too I suppose, in time for lunch.'

'Neat,' and 'Choice,' they said from the phone and the extension.

In Room Four we sat on baby chairs with our knees in our chins. The little grandkids weren't overawed at all by the big children with their recorders, glokenspiels, tambourines, xylophones, bells, chimes, triangles, drums, shakers and clappers. While we waited I had this idea of changing all the first letters of instruments to bring about decorders, blokenspiels, pylophones, bambourines, pells, himes, hiangles, brums, takers and lappers. It pleased me for a time, then thought I'd better concentrate because the little grandkids were coming to a high pitch, taking

no notice of the teacher bossing. They wanted to go outside,
wanted their faces painted, wanted a pony ride, a hot dog. I was
happy with their lack of silence.

'After, after.'

'Later, later.'

'Sit down.'

'Sit on a little chair.'

There is a girl. She was sitting on a little chair and could not
speak because she had only wrong language to use. There was a
voice. 'Stand up when I speak to you. Answer me, answer me at
once,' it said.

Keri, who is wearing two dresses, and Rawiri, who has a T-shirt
on over the top of a sweat shirt, are rolling their eyes at me trying
not to show too much of their importance. It's not me that makes
them weird. Pit-a-pat, pit-a-pat hear the sound of falling rain,
pit-a-pat, pit-a-pat, on my window pane. Sometimes in strange
surroundings you can forget who you are. Drink to me only with
thine eyes, Hine e Hine, softlee, softlee, catchee monkee. Well,
not so strange, just not an everyday environment these days. I
feel fat and forgetful surrounded by miniatures.

As well as the real children there are cutouts of children
standing by cutouts of houses, pasted against crayoned and
painted roads, telegraph poles, trees, flowers and hills. Some of
the cutout children are clothed in skirts and trousers of coloured
cotton and corduroy, while others have clothes that have been
painted or felt-tipped on. Some have wool hair. In the thick
brushwork of sky there are two smiling suns, a crescent of moon,
a stick of lightning and a fall of rain.

The opposite wall is top to toe in stories that begin with 'I
am'. I am laughing. I am crying. I am jumping. I am Superman.

I am at the grandmother's house. I am Michelangelo. I am at home. I am. I am going to McDonald's.

Me? I am forgetful among the cushions and story books, blocks and dress-ups, mini house with its furniture dishes pots and pans all in smallness. There are collections of leaves, twigs, stones, shells, buttons, containers, plastic spoons, icecream sticks, egg shells, cartons and cards. And then all the hangings — litter mobiles, story mobiles, light catchers, wind catchers and instructions in suspension. Benches, screens, dividers. You can forget, become part of a collage where you may see yourself stuck — button-eyed, stick-legged, hands like sated ticks. Hang if you don't remember.

There is a girl. She was picking at her muddy skin, picking, picking until the worms appeared. 'Fleas and maggots, fleas and maggots, mungie mungie typo,' the voices sang.

Coins of faces, the striker pausing, the taut space between the tick and the brum, the notes recording, the tapering pells and himes. I make a cup of my left hand and with the other, clap over this hollow that I have made. I'm proud of my echoey ovations and my eyeing grandchildren.

Last time I was in a school was when I went up to the college to try and persuade the timetabler to allow Pere to take the subjects he wanted. His groupings were wrong and timetabling wouldn't allow it, I was told.

'Is this school for kids or is it for timetables?' I asked, trying to be smart.

'He has to select from each group, take subjects that fit together — like Maths and Science,' the timetabler said.

'Is this school for kids or is it for subjects?' I asked, getting bumptious.

'Art, Mathematics, Agriculture and Maori don't go

together,' he told me. 'They're in different groupings.' He wanted to give me a printout to prove what he had said was true, but I didn't want to look at any printout. I could feel myself losing ground and didn't need that shown to me in black and white.

'It's a weird combination, Art, Maths, Agriculture and Maori,' Mr Timetable said, smiling, walking me to the foyer trying to think of something joking and friendly to say to cheer me. 'What a weird son you've got. He'll have to make up his mind whether he wants to be an artist, an economist, a farmer or . . .' His smile left him and he blushed.

'A Maori,' I said. It shook him. I felt triumphant. I left.

The instruments are passed along to the ends of the rows where prefects disappear them into cupboards. Some kids leave and others come. Keri, who is smooth and beautiful and reminds me of midsummer plums, and Rawiri, who is thin and gawky with teeth and eyes that are too big for him, go to join a group out in the porch ready for the kapa haka items. Rawiri has his Michael doll tucked under one arm. Through the glass in the door I can see Rose Mei holding a guitar by its neck. She's shushing the kids and has a worried expression.

In they come singing, forming rows, synchronising. I feel guilty seeing the work that has gone into it. I could've come and helped Rose once a week if it wasn't for my resolution. She's worked on head and foot actions as well as arm and hand. Eyes too. The kids are good — know how to make it all happen between them and us. Good voices. The baby kids on their baby chairs are tranced.

'You missed it,' I said to two dreadlocked, bearded, sun-glassed uncles, 'the orchestra and the kapa haka. You would've been proud of your nephew and niece.' They have with them Belle and Janes and enough tomato-sauced sausages on sticks for everyone.

'What did you think?' asked Michael doll.

'It was great. Tell Rawiri it was great,' I said to Michael doll.

'Did you hear that, Rawiri?'

'I heard.'

'Choice.'

'We want.'

'We want.'

'A pony ride.'

'Face paint.'

'Face paint.'

'Face.'

'Face.'

There is a girl. She was backed up against a garage wall spitting blood and stones.

'So tell me why you're wearing two dresses.'

'It's a dress and a skirt,' Keri says. 'A dress underneath and a skirt over top because I couldn't make up my mind.'

'Okay then, why a shirt over a jersey?'

'Because,' Michael doll replies, jigging into my face, 'if he puts the shirt on underneath the jersey no one will be able to read what it says — Save Our Planet.' How great my grand-children are, how they save me. The realisation is debilitating. A pool of warm water I am.

'Here's fifteen bucks,' I say to Jemma. 'Get them all face paint, pony rides, whatever.'

'We don't need fifteen.'

'Take it, spend it on something. I don't want to take it home again.'

Soon we have a batman, a spiderwoman, a clown, two ninja turtles and another, I don't know what — a star maybe, going to queue up for ponies.

In the hall I am thin and alert. It's the kind of place where I often find myself in touch with me. But I don't find myself among the knitted dolls, embroidered bookmarks, lace covered tissue boxes, tulle bath cleaners, oven mitts and patchwork aprons. No.

I'm not there with potted apple mint, peppers, rosemary, garlic chives, lemon balm or parsley — nor with the cyclamen, fuchsia, rhipsalidopsis. African violets? I remember that they like warm water, steamy rooms, but I refuse to be interested in their juicy hands, their gentian faces and it's no use them looking at me winking little yellow eyes. Look here, Violet, you'd be sorry if I did. I'd neglect you, forget to water and steam bath you. You'd die.

I leave quickly. There are five dollars I have to spend on something but not on bonnets, bootees, matinee jackets, bibs, feeders, leggings, stretch-n-grows. Save me from all this.

Not dried flowers either, or straw ladies, pot pourri, lavender bags, perfumed sachets, pine cone owls, shell mice and turtles, driftwood families. Bark arrangements — which could be what they're meant to be, or could be Bach pieces, or a group of singing dogs. I'm pleased with myself about all that.

Most of the produce has gone. I could've, if there was a large banana cake, taken it home, chopped it up into square hunks and we'd have gobbled into it. But there's only one small cake left, lemon, with yellow sprinkles on white icing under a slime of gladwrap. There are a few bits of ginger crunch, a jar of marmalade, a bottle of pickle and an old cabbage. Hump.

But also there are a few baskets of sweets — fudge, coconut ice and burnt toffee. The baskets have been made from cut-in-half packets, cornflour and lasagne boxes that have been covered with fringes of crêpe paper. I could get one each for the ninjas, etc. But the parents won't like it because sweets'll make the kids hyper. They're already hyper so what's the difference?

But I resist. Anyway, the baskets are inferior. With a little more knowledge the basketmakers could've made vertical snips in the strips of crêpe, at five centimetre intervals, and using a knitting needle could've rolled and crimped the cut edges into petal shapes before layering them around the little boxes. For extra class and variegation they could've put two colours together before making the curls. I feel like telling someone this.

White elephant is more like it. Getting warm. What about a mouli, a jug element, toast racks, *Boy's Own Annual*, peeing boy decanter, firescreens, paua shell frogs, plaster girl with cat, handlebars, Platters records, pop beads, bar mirrors, rolls of wallpaper. Not really. Not even a Japanese fan? No, not really.

Missing from all this is Jemma and me's stall that we could've had, of weaving, to bring a different ethnicity to all this. Flax kono, we could've made and sold for three dollars each, and in them lemons, tomatoes and beans. Could've done three or four potato kits too which seem to be bigtime at the moment and were snatched in the first ten minutes at the Molesworth Street Market Day. Jemma could've done earrings, bracelets, head-bands maybe. Even Keri, even Rawiri. I'm so glad to have succeeded in not having a stall, just as I'm pleased with myself not to have deprived Rose of slogging it out each week alone with the kapa haka group. I'm happy to have snubbed winking violet.

But pre-loved clothes? Oh. There's a knitted shawl of apple green that I can see could be made into a dress for a little girl, like Tiria, who at the moment is being a heavenly body on horse-back. There are coats that could be made into shirts, skirts that could be trousers, jerseys that could be hats and gloves and slippers, or other jerseys. If I was a proper grandmother. But I'm thin and wide awake to myself now, determined not to buy up unwanted items that I will never remake into wanted.

Anyway there are perfect handknits that don't need remaking into anything. They are already it, yes. So I rummage through to find the right sizes, not that anyone seems to worry about sizes these days, except for big enough. Yes. yes. I stuff the woollies into a plastic bag that the keeper gives me, feeling excited and marvellous, and with only two dollars left to get rid of.

I queue up for tea and the fortune teller, telling the tea sellers that I don't drink tea but I'm keen on having the leaves read.

'We'll tip most of it out,' they say. 'Then you can just take a sip and blow on it a few times. That should do the trick.'

'You do believe, don't you,' the leaf reader said, 'that I'm going to tell you something important and of value to yourself?'

'Well I . . . um . . . had two dollars . . .'

'Tip it upside down on the saucer. Give it a turn or two.'

She is wearing two dresses too. The underneath one is floral crimplene with a scooped neckline. Over the top of it she has a gauzy green gown with a dippy hem which is caught across the middle of her by a large glass brooch. She has a round, kind face.

'You know,' she said, 'it's interesting isn't it, but someone like you just has to learn to use her time. So many commitments. It's always been a problem hasn't it? But let's not call it that, a problem. It's the difficulty of always being interested in everything, always wanting to know, have a hand in, have a say. And it's the competence that you get after a while. It's all right being good at things, being interested, getting involved, but then it traps you. You get pulled this way and that until it's too much. Too many demands. Well you'll have to leave some of it for others now. Delegate, you know.'

Who is this gauzy woman?

'Otherwise how will you ever be able to get on with this new undertaking. You need the time for yourself. It's difficult, isn't it, when you're not used to it, to take time?

'And there's a show, or something like that, that you'll attend. It'll have meaning for you, something misty.'

Who can this be?
So gauze and green,
With glass
Centring eye.

'Now what about the past?'

What indeed? Her old, kind face is blotchy — red, white and purple. It is an attractive face with old teeth that jut forward. Her eyes bulge in the way that buck-toothed people's eyes often do. Her fingers caress the cup as she turns it onto my past.

'Harp music. There's something here about harp music. Is that something you enjoy, harp music?'

'No, not harp in particular. I don't think. No I've never . . .'

'That's strange, because there's something here to do with . . . harp music. Definitely. So let's think about that. Perhaps it might be that something to do with harp music will bring forward a memory. It could be that that memory will hold something of significance for you, you know, help you to know or understand something. About yourself, to do with you. Because it's difficult to remember sometimes, you get involved, distracted, keep moving out to the edges, forget the core and lose the way back. Yes I think so. About you. Anyway think about that, about the harp music and it'll give you a boost, you'll see.'

All right I will, beautiful woman.

'Well that's it and it's been interesting I must say. It's been good, hasn't it, for you. Something about now, advice for you about all your involvements and giving some of it away, but you're already trying to, aren't you? All you need is the encouragement. Then something that you'll do in the future, the near future I'd say, attend a show of some sort. And something from the past which might be the most important of all, bringing a memory you know, to do with harp music.'

The ninjas are arguing about which one of them is

Michelangelo. All of them, ninjas, spiderpeople, cats, batmen and heavenly bodies, are wearing odd socks because they're weird. Parents too.

'If you all line up,' I say, 'and look down, you'll see the mates of socks on each other, then you could all swap and have proper pairs.'

No one says anything. I can tell they're wondering why I would think they would ever want to do such a thing.

The Michelangelos are still at it. 'I always wanted to be Tom Mix,' I say. 'We had beachwood guns and we shanks's ponied along the sand being cowboys.'

They are underawed, even Keri, though she smiles and nods to humour me.

'Why don't you both be Michelangelo then?'

'I don't want to now, I want to be Raphael.'

'No I'm Raphael.'

'Is that all you bought?' I am asked in genuine surprise.

'How come you haven't bought a whole stall?'

'Whole hall?'

'Whole school?'

'It's not all. I got some stuff from the tealeaf woman for two dollars.'

'Well how come?' asked Jemma after I'd told.

'Don't know. She saw it in the tealeaves.'

'That's weird. I mean how did she know about the research and stuff?'

'Undertaking, she called it.'

'Sounds like shoplifted gruts.'

'And then when she said that about the misty show I thought of the exhibition that's coming up — that brochure . . .'

'That painting on the front of it. All the tipuna with their sombre eyeballs looking out through mists of skies and mists of scapes.'

'Scapes' is weird.

Kids are all upside down on the playground bars and so are their father-uncles, coins dropping out of their pockets. They're singing sad songs.

Does that make us all crazy? Is it me that makes them weird? Is the whole world wairangi, haurangi, porangi? Well hell! We've turned all these things against ourselves, haven't we? Look at the state of water now. Think what the wind is likely to bring to our lungs these days. Think of the big cloud coming — long, cold darknesses and having to live forever underground.

What? Going on a downer? But I reach.

'Thank goodness for woollies,' I say. I pull them all out as we make our way to the cars. There's a stripy jumper, an off-white cable knit jacket, a brown cardigan with duffle buttons, a grey jersey with soldiers back and front, a shell-stitched matinee jacket, a multi-coloured poncho, a blue hat with pompoms and a red hat with green ear flaps.

'Hup, two, three, four,' says the soldier batman kid, marching in the new old jersey. And hup, two, three, four the others repeat, marching along behind.

I decide to put some thought to harp music, but realise I need to get home to do the thinking, it's no use trying in amongst the hup, two, threes. I'll have to get rid of everyone, or if they come home with me I'll have to go to bed and let them get on with cooking stuff.

But when we get to the cars they all slam and toot away in different directions, all the ninjas, soldiers etc, swapped or given back to their part owners and shareholders.

So then I am alone and offended, facing an empty house. If I had banana cake they'd have come.

Anyway harp music. I needed to think about just that, if only to keep winters off me.

For a long time I walk about the darkening house touching

the walls, the furniture, the switches, sometimes switching them —on off, on off, on off. Round inside me. Eyes closed, knowing that I know every corner of this house.

Or do I?

Keeping in touch, and knowing that I won't do anything else until I know what it is
                    to do
              with harp music.

And then she comes, the girl, from somewhere. From my hip. She has short black plaits and is wearing a school tunic and a white long-sleeved blouse. She looks at me then moves away and I see her running down a hillside dodging the stumps and stones, horse dung and thistles, stopping by an old fence near to her house.

It's a wire fence, but not the usual paddock fence of post and batten with five strands of number eight. It does have cross strands, double the usual number, but it has vertical strands as well, making a high fence of wire rectangles. The wire is much finer than number eight and has become rusty and brittle. There are places where it has broken, and several places where it has been mended by twisting and tying the strands together.

The girl stops running when she comes to the fence and walks along beside it bending or reaching up, to turn the twists and ties. She is setting up the orchestra in which she will be one of the players, and turning the knobs of the giant radio over which the music will be heard.

When she is satisfied that all the preparations have been completed she sits in the long grass close to the fence, rests a cheek against it and puts one arm through. Then with both hands she begins to pluck and stroke the strings, and it happens as it has happened before, the music.

The music is all around walking, then running, swirling, climbing, and she is part of the playing. There is an eye of moon in the sky and a journey down to the sea walking on rocks in a dress that is yellow. One part of the music has the beat of the sea. There's smoke from a far chimney going to the eye in the sky.

And she is lifting too, lifting to the moon-eye and looking down over water and rocks and trees and paddocks, but at the same time she is playing the music. There are people with faces like wide bowls, looking up at her.

After a time she descends and the music is fading. Soon it has all gone but she knows it is her own.

She walks beside the fence again turning the switches of her radio, and when everything is done she comes, leggy and laughing and pleased with herself, running towards me.

Chain of Events

Maria hung her jacket behind the door and put on her smock, ready to dish up. Mrs Jackson came in and told her that there'd been some cutting back and that from now on clients would not be allowed second helpings.

The door opened and the first lot came in, shuffling, stumbling, clenching teeth, flapping an arm, dragging a leg, making noises. The ones who were able lined up with their plates, while the client-aids sat the others down at the tables to have their meals brought to them.

Maria began serving out and it wasn't a bad day because all the clients arrived at the tables without accidents, sat down and began chomping the food which was lukewarm so they wouldn't burn themselves. They used plastic spoons with which they could do no harm, shovelling and swallowing.

While they were eating the mince and vegetables Maria dished out the puddings and put them ready on the counter. She pushed the trolley out front so that clients and helpers could scrape and stack their first lot of dishes and put their cutlery in the basin of soapy water. After that they could get the puddings which they would eat quickly so they could come up for seconds.

Darlene with the rashes, who was always first, stood up, splitting her dress under both armpits, jolting the table and making the dishes jump while her chair went sliding. She came stamping up to the counter, looking pleased, calling, 'Maria, Maria.'

Maria had to tell Darlene that Mrs Jackson had said that she wasn't allowed to give anyone seconds now, that there wasn't any more because it was all dished up the first time. She had to show Darlene the empty dish and tell her over and over until she understood.

Then Darlene threw her bowl, punched her fist through a window and fell down with a wide spike of glass through her wrist. When one of the client-aids pulled the piece of glass out blood began spurting everywhere and there was loud noise with plates and chairs falling and people shouting.

The ambulance came and Darlene was taken to hospital while the other clients, laughing and crying, were taken away so that the cleaning up could be done. Security was sent for and a few old boards were nailed up over the window.

That night Maria had nightmares in which she was spooning up bloody tapioca while Darlene stood by her laughing and laughing, both arms severed.

When she went to work the next day and asked about Darlene, Mrs Jackson said, 'Still in hospital, good job, serve the silly bitch right, always throwing her weight around upsetting the place. Pity she didn't put her head through.'

Maria hung her jacket behind the door and put on her smock ready to serve the food as the first ones came through the door.

Cardigan of Roses

She came in and said, as though she thought he might be interested, 'You know I could read by the time I went to school. It was my brother, went blind in an accident when he was twelve, Bernie. Him. Made me read to him. Newspapers or anything. If I didn't know what it was he'd say spell it. I'd spell, then he'd tell me the word. That's how I learned. Every day after school he'd be waiting for me on the back steps. In the kitchen if it was cold, the fire going, and he'd get me to. Hours sometimes until our mother said that's enough you haven't even changed your clothes, fed the chooks, got the milk.'

He wished she'd shut up, or wished he could go out, but it was already dark. If he went off somewhere and fell he'd have a hell of a job getting himself back up, and anyway where was there to go? Or if he went out to the shed what would he do? Sit there looking.

'That's why at school I had to go to a higher class, because of the reading. Started school late. Seven. But I caught up with my age group, easy. Even passed some. But when I was eleven I had to stop school. The teachers wanted me to go to college and I would've if my mother didn't get sick. It had to be me to look after her because the others had jobs. Had to hold on to their jobs because our father was dead and we needed it. Bernie didn't work, well couldn't, but he helped with some things. Sawed wood but he couldn't chop. It was sand. You wouldn't think would you. Sand in the eyes and ending up blind. Total.'

If only she would watch television or listen to her radio

stations like she used to all the time. Maddening. It was since he'd lost his leg she seemed to think she had to talk all the time, tell her life story as if he hadn't heard it. Or was it because he was always there now, one-legged, trapped, and half of most of his fingers gone so he couldn't tinker with parts and cars.

And just because of that, just because he couldn't, she'd had the cheek to ring Jerome and tell him to come and take the cars away. But he'd put a stop to that. I'm not dead yet. He'd told Jerome to leave the cars where they were but he could come any time and get whatever parts he wanted. He liked Jerome coming, a few revs before he turned the motor off and jumped out, bent at the knees and elbows, like ready to spring up. But he didn't spring up. Jerome stayed bent. Sometimes it wasn't to get anything, just to show him a part, like the voltage regulator from a '34 pick-up that he brought over last week. They looked and talked.

Anyway today he'd got Jerome to do something for him — the post and the bit of fence that he'd wanted to do years ago but kept putting off. Now it was done.

'Our mother was tall and I was small when I was eleven. I helped her round, bathroom, everything. Did the washing, cooking, most of it, till fifteen, then she died. Everybody was gone away by then, my sisters and relatives. Had jobs in the city. When they came back to our mother's funeral they reckoned I could go and stay with them and get work too. There were good jobs and the pay was all right. I would've but Bernie didn't want to.

'Anyway I got work near home. Waitress, after that barmaid. Two years waitress and ten years barmaid. One summer, when I was eighteen, they stuck me in the queen carnival beauty contest. I was Miss Dinn's Post and it was a penny a vote. Well we had copper trails out in the hotel lobby and up the stairs, raffle or two on the bar, Bernie round shaking his collection box and sisters and cousins sending a bit from wherever they were.

'There was a display board in town with our names across the top, well not our own names — Miss Denham's Bakery, Miss Oakley Bay, Miss Dinn's Post and so on. The board was numbered up and there were arrows showing how many votes. In the end I was second runner-up.'

All day long. There was only a certain amount of time in a day that he could thump about on crutches, or get wheeled around. Or Katty driving them on Sundays. Nowhere, just using up petrol around the bays. Sometimes in the winter he went with Toss to the park if there was a game on. A couple of times a week he'd lean on the fence and wait for the Next Doors to come home, the Monster family carting their bags of groceries. Supermarket Woman and her supermarket kids. He'd give them some jaw about their driveway, about the boundary. Now and again Jerome came. But it wasn't all the time there was something to do.

'He got round all right. Being blind didn't stop him. Come to the bar and stay there until it was time for me to knock off and we'd walk home. I still used to read to him. That was our thing, that was the thing we had, this reading. Until he got married which I didn't like. I didn't expect that. I thought I might one day but not him, and used to wonder what he'd do if I wanted to. But it was him. I didn't like her and I thought he might be sorry, have no one to read. I was right about that too, she never. But he learned braille, got talking books. After I moved up here they got him a typewriter. He always wrote to me, typewritten and no mistakes.'

Most of the time nothing. If only she'd stop he wouldn't mind telling her about how he'd put one across the Next Doors, how he'd got Jerome to dig the hole, told him how to mix the concrete, put the post in and put the boards up. After that he'd told Jerome he could take the Vee Dub. Jerome had another Vee

Dub at home and was going to swap motors, make one good one but anyway he could hear something, someone. There was something going on now, outside, someone coming thank God. Someone at the door, can't you hear?

'Two legs, one leg, no legs, you needn't think you're getting away with this,' said Supermarket Woman in the doorway, filling it. 'You can get that post out of my driveway, get that bit of fence, if you call it a fence, down, or I'm calling the police.'

'Call them, call them. I got a few things I want to point out.'

'Don't you come busting in here yelling at a man, sick, like that.' Life Story. He wished she'd shut up, keep her nose out.

'Sick doesn't stop him thieving, one-legged doesn't stop him running off at the mouth hanging over the fence into my place.'

'Call them, go on. I'll show them where you been running over my property the last ten years.'

'I know where my boundary is. I know where my peg is.'

'Didn't see no peg.'

'You rooted it out, likely.'

'Yourself likely, because it didn't suit.'

'I'm telling you, get that post and those half-rotten boards off my driveway or that's it.' Standing over him, cheeks red and wattling, a sausagey finger stabbing air in front of his face. Stab stab, yab yab. He wanted to laugh.

'You'll find yourself in court.' Where he could be heroic with his missing bits — police, lawyers, judges, the media.

'I'll look forward to that,' he said, meaning it.

But what? Life Story was picking up an end of manuka from the fire. Here's a go. Swishing it up and back over her shoulder, sparks arcing. 'Get out, get out, or you'll get it, coming here and threatening the disabled.'

Now Supermarket was backing out, backing down the steps, down the track. The sparks rainbowed, then the chunk flew.

Prickling stars, looping and hurtling through the dark, until the piece met Supermarket's shoulder and shied off to hit the shed wall where the stars busted all over the place.

'I'm getting the police, you're nuts,' over the shoulder damage as she departed down the dark side of the path, orange rain still falling and flames beginning to lick along the skeleton of runner bean vines and to chew on the sill of the shed. Here was something. Burn, burn.

'We're burning,' said Life Story hurrying inside for water in a bucket, running out, hurling it, running in again out again, missing by miles, the flames growing and spreading. He enjoyed it for a while then he thought he'd better tell her.

'Hit it with a bag,' he said. 'Most of it misses when you throw. Most of it's on you. A bag, a coat, anything like that — your cardigan of roses. Wet it.'

She began to unbutton her cardigan which had gone the shape of her bowl-shaped back, her bundles-of-paper breasts, and which was dipped and pointy in front where she'd pushed her fingers down into the corners of the pockets. Rows of blue roses on a black garden her cardigan was. The top row of roses nodded to the right, the next row to the left, and so on down. Each blue rose had its own black space to nod across, making you want to count them.

He watched her dip the garment in the bucket and begin slapping it against the wall, and when the fire was out he felt disappointed. She dumped the cardigan in the bucket and came inside. He could hear her showering. Soon she'd be in telling again how she used to be Miss High and Mighty this, Miss High and Mighty that. Reading and every bloody thing.

If they'd gone up in flames that would've been something. Flying out the ranchsliders in his wheelchair he would've. All lit up. Fire engines and ambulances wa wa, wa wa, wa wa, and too late. Hey, there were these old wire toasting racks once, that you could put a slice of bread on and hold over the embers. If there was too much flame the bread would burn on to the wires and it would be impossible to get it off in one piece. Pick and scrape and the whole thing messed up.

That's what he'd have been by the time the hoses arrived. Burnt toast. Frizzed to his chair and having to be picked and chipped off, that'd be something.

Life Story coming.

'After he got married I came up here. I had no trouble getting a job because I had references. Bernie shifted away too, to be nearer to the Institute. He did all right, Bernie. He started off helping at the Institute and later got to be one of the top people there. He got on.

'He loved the fair, I remember. We used to go together. He'd take the wheel of the dodgem cars and I'd tell him turn right, turn left and so on. I'd even try and tell him how to throw the hooplas and he got a red dish once.

'There was this game I was good at. I had it worked out. It was a race seeing who could get their monkey to the top of the pole first, working a lever which popped the ball in and sent the monkey up notch by notch. I worked out the right speed to flick the lever and kept winning these boxes of chocolates. They were off mostly, bleached and musty.'

Stopped.

What's up? Sitting staring into the fire as though she really is nuts. Thinking about what? What? 'So what?'

So get me away from the half-people, from eyes that can't see and I am the eyes, from half-death where I am the crutch under the arm, the decipherer of words that limp off the side of a tongue out of the side of a mouth, jumbled and dribbled. From the part-people with fingers and toes missing, a foot going, then one leg and the other likely to follow. Buried piece by piece until there are only heads in rows, open-mouthed, turning from side to side.

'What?'

'He liked the ping pong clowns, I didn't have to instruct him very much because he'd do it all by touch and sound. But he needed me to describe the clowns to him so that he could choose. 'They're all the same,' I'd say sometimes, but it wasn't true. He knew. There were always these little differences — a piece chipped off, scratches in the paint, someone's initials, a sadder or happier expression, something in the eyes.'

Load of bullshit.

'He'd place his left hand on the cheek of the clown, and when he thought it was the right time, pop the balls in. He'd score just as good as anyone else. We'd stay there playing until closing time. Sometimes I thought of leaving him there but I never did.'

Sweet Trees

'It's her.'

'Her who?'

'You know. Her. That one that we . . .'

'That one? Is that her, the one sitting you can hardly see?'

'That's her.'

'Well, I mean, I mean, crikey.'

'Same here. That's what I think too.'

'We didn't mean it . . . like that.'

'Course not.'

'It was supposed to be, you know, fun. And she's . . .'

'Miserable.'

'It was him, that Fantail stuffed things up.'

'Shouldn't've let him come.'

'Stuffing around, stuffing things up every time.'

'I mean we could've had them just meet . . . somewhere nice, in trees, ferns, by the creek, the two of them. Summer. Cool places. We could've watched out for them.'

'Instead of that Piwaka has to experiment, go exotic.'

'He's a pain in the bum.'

'That giggle of his gets on my wing.'

'And now look.'

'Poor thing all by herself sitting on a, on a what?'

'On a nothing, a white square.'

'You can hardly see her.'

'Fading into it.'

'She used to laugh and dance.'

'Used to wear sun and flowers.'
'What's her name again?'
'Maneta.'
'What'll we do?'
'We got to go there, do something.'
'It's a long way.'
'We got to.'

I was walking in the sea with Kata. I don't mean strolling barefoot, paddling, cooling off along the shore like lovers or friends. We were heading shorewards (so I thought at first), in water that was waist deep. We were dressed as though for a picnic, perhaps an outing with children, perhaps summer shopping, Kata wearing a plain blue tee and long cotton shorts with patterns and colours crashing together. I wore a hand-painted tee of sun and flowers and green denim shorts. We both had our belt bags strapped round our middles and we both wore sandals, deeply interested in our conversation. There was something in the air.

The water was a charcoal colour because of the solid cloud overhead, and so smooth that the ripples caused by our movement had the density of dark rope. Except for the edge of cold that the water held, it was a blunt day. It seemed there were no previous circumstances to our being there, no world record attempts at flying off a jetty, no raft racing, boating accidents, whale rescue, parachute drop. There were no other people. Only Kata, me.

And it wasn't until we turned to look at each other that we became surprised. I didn't know until we talked about it later what it was that surprised Kata, but what astounded me was that I saw his eyes were tiny silver propellers, spinning. His heart was a small pull-start motor driving a belt connected to groin sprockets and rod. I could see all this despite the dark water.

I noticed that although we were facing shore we weren't going anywhere, walking but not making any progress. I didn't mind. I was happy talking about our lives. He asked me if we were on a treadmill, but I didn't think so. Treadmills are grey and grinding, bone-breaking. They crush broken bone to grit and powder. Treadmills are bleak eternity. 'We're on top of the world,' I said, 'walking and turning it. If it wasn't for you and me everything would be at a standstill,' and I could see that he believed me. He turned his face towards the sky and yahooed a blast of ringing springs.

Here they were, all these springs, golden, dropping into the sea about us, cutting and slicing, making their own sharp light. I knew then that I loved him.

'We shouldn't've let him talk us into it.'

'It's that mouth of his.'

'Making everything sound okay.'

'Next thing you're going along going along going along, letting him.'

'And I mean, when we left there it was like it was all right. The two of them, both rapt.'

'So rapt you'd think there was enough . . .'

'Rapture . . .'

'For a lifetime.'

'We should've stuck to the original plan. Set them down in a place we know. A forest.'

'Come to a swamp we could've led them off some other way.'

'Cold, could've feathered them.'

'Dark, could've twittered them down till daylight.'

'No, that one just barged ahead. Us just going along like halfwits.'

'It's that giggle giggle giggle of his.'

'And that fan. Flicker flicker flicker. You got your mind on that and the next thing he's up to tricks.'

'The sea? Crikey, it's the last place.'

'Wouldn't last half a day there. You and me.'

'Or him.'

'What a place.'

'Didn't even let seagull know we were coming.'

'Embarrassing.'

'Flitting into someone else's country like that.'

'Pleasing ourselves.'

'Anyway, where's the other one. Him. The one she was in love with?'

'Well, aa, I think that could be him.'

'What? That, that kind of, shadow, on that black square?'

'Mm.'

'Oh it's not fair.'

'We got to do something.'

'Got to have a plan.'

'And this time . . .'

'Don't let him get flick of it.'

I was walking in the sea with Maneta, the sea so dark that it could have been oil. No. It had the feel and smell of sea.

There were only the two of us and we were talking about our lives, not pausing to wonder how we came to be doing what we were doing, or why. We'd never met before. We weren't dressed for swimming. It wasn't summer. We didn't seem to be going anywhere but we were talking and talking.

She turned to me and I saw that her eyes were watches. Not watchers, watches. They were two old-time watches with the backs taken off, all the little wheels and cogs turning, the balances dipping and wheeling like tiny fairground rides, studded with jewels of soft colours. And I knew I was in love. Hey, I'm in love with a woman with ticking eyes. The water wasn't becoming shallower. We weren't getting any nearer to shore.

'Do you think we're on a treadmill?' I asked, thinking it not a time to speak of love, 'because we don't seem to be going anywhere.'

'I thought,' she said, 'that maybe we had the world at our feet, that we were here, walking, turning it.' Then she laughed and out of her mouth came a shower of bluestone drops, crystal prisms, silver pins.

'Half out of our element?' I asked.

'Or half in,' she said. I saw that her heart was a clock face, with clock hands spinning. Was she in love? From the clock face hung a pendulum lodging a bright disc between her thighs. Did I have X-ray eyes?

'Surprise, surprise.'

'What're you doing here?'

'Just looking.'

'Having a listen too, I bet.'

'Sticky beak.'

'Sticky? No, I'm no sucker, that's Tui and her lot you're thinking of. I have dinner on the wing, just like yous.'

'Well were you listening or what?'

'Did you hear or not?'

'Course I did.'

'And?'

'And what?'

'The whole thing's a mess.'

'Ti, ti, ti, ti.'

'Look at her, look at him.'

'Kss ss ss ss.'

'They had no chance.'

'What do you mean no chance? It was up to them, wasn't it?'

'You left them.'

'Me? You mean we. We left them.'

'All right, we. But what did we know about storms, cold, rust, unfriendly fish?'

'Ss ss ss, kss, kss, ti ti.'

'All that gimmicky mechanical stuff.'

'All that "atmosphere". How were they to know? How were we to know?'

'Gullible yous. I mean yous were on the spot when Maui got his comeuppance, saw the lot. You could've learned from that.'

'You blew it then, that's for sure.'

'Depends how you look at it.'

'Shouldn't trust you at all, Fantail.'

'Why do yous then?'

Our lives? Well what I told Kata went like this. This is the shortened version. It wasn't the life I wanted, but it was lively.

I remember standing on a floor being shaken in the dark by my mother, clothes pulling over my head. Beside me Rori, beside him Mariana, beside her Georgie Boy, being stuffed into clothes.

Then out on the footpaths being pulled along, the string of us, by our mother. There was a boy in a story who went to the butcher for sausages, and instead of carrying them in a better way he trailed them behind him on a string and was chased by puppies. That story always reminds me of that night when I was a sausage, mother hurrying along pulling with one hand. In her other hand she carried and dragged a stuffed bag.

It was an empty road and we kept to the dark side of it. There were no street lights but there was a moon side. We kept out of sight of the moon.

The string broke. It had to because Georgie Boy was little. She had to pick him up. Rori and I had to drag the bag, but try not to drag it, hold it up, as if we could. Mariana wanted to dare to sit on the road and cry because Georgie Boy was being carried, but it wasn't the sort of situation where she could do it. She could've been left sitting there in the dark. So only a whimper now and then came from her, hurrying to keep up, carrying nothing.

Out in the moonlight we crossed a road and a little bridge and came to the edge of town where the streets were lit and empty. There was a taxi. She pushed us in. 'Railway station please,' she said, and off we went enough miles for us to be asleep by the time the wheels stopped at daylight with our mother saying, 'I haven't got any money, you can have my ring as long as you give me change.' Think of that — 'as long as you give me change.' She never was a broken woman.

'Forget it,' the taxi driver said, looking peeved, and put us all on the platform with the bag.

In the train there was not a word spoken between our mother and the gummy guard that walked through the carriage that for a while we had to ourselves. He took a look and went by because of my mother's face, the way her lips were together, her nose haughty, her eyes turned away. The way she pretended distraction holding the arm of Georgie Boy, squeezing her knees about him standing between them. The guard went by, whistling in the flap-lipped way of people without teeth, clicking clippers. He didn't look at us at all after that.

In the afternoon we were stringing along again but slower, in the town where we'd got off the train. We'd eaten the half packet of biscuits from the bag and Georgie Boy was crying for food because he was too young to know better. Mariana had to know better.

We went from pub to pub. One and two wouldn't have us, not kids, not a woman with only a ring. But in the third there was a woman with a smoked face, a smoked bobble of yellow hair on her forehead while the rest of her hair was white and short above the ears. Smoked teeth. 'Tell you what I'll sack the new girl because she's useless but pretty enough to get a job anywhere,' she said. 'You try it for a month. It's rooms, bathrooms, lounge, hallways, bar, kitchen and dining room. Cleaning and laundry with cooking Saturdays. Board and keep for you and the kids, a room with two beds and a cot. No noise. No kids in the bar or lounge or hanging round the hallways and stairs.'

It wasn't the life I wanted, sitting in a bedroom or out walking the footpaths with Rori, Mariana and Georgie Boy, or doing out rooms and taking turns with Rori to go to school. But it was better than before. No screaming, our mother being throttled in the dark. It was lively, and what our mother said was true, that people were good.

But I knew that later I would look for someone to tell it all to, to make my life different, not thinking it would happen suddenly in such a way.

'My life has been lived in one place,' I said to Maneta, in one house with a mother who hid a bottle in every room, a father who worked nights — four to midnight, a brother three years younger.

'I wanted an ordinary life, which I knew about through spying, listening, and watching television. I knew about families and their three meals a day, their hot night meals sitting at a table. Not that we didn't have food. My father shopped before he went to work, for bread, pies, milk, tea, biscuits and apples. Sometimes he'd buy us clothes which were always different to the clothes that other boys wore. Before we came home from school he'd be gone.

'I knew from listening that there were kids who took other kids home to play after school, who had friends to stay on Saturdays and went on holidays together. There were families, some without fathers, some without mothers, who had parties and barbecues and had aunts and uncles and cousins that came. They had food, wine and guitars like the people next door.

'Something else I knew was that children and parents, or grandparents, sometimes had long conversations about the cost of things, the olden days, the legs of flies. "Flies taste food with their hairy legs," said Craig at school. "They walk on stuff and know if it tastes good. They've got sticky feet and that's how they walk upside down."

' "How do you know?" I asked him.

' "Because last night I had a conversation about it with my father." There were families with jokes and riddles and Ludo.

'Our mother had a morning job. It was making morning tea. She dressed up for it, tweezed her eyebrows, put her makeup on, a skirt and blouse, her best shoes. Bottle in her pocket. She'd be fuzzed by the time we came home from school, indistinct, smeared, lipstick seeping into the creases at the edges of her mouth. Drawling. But always loving in her own way.

'We were all right. My spying and listening had also told me there were children who were beaten every day, who were locked in cupboards, lived in the streets, starved. We were all right but it wasn't ordinary, or lively, and my brother and I always had a secret and a silence to carry everywhere.

'It wasn't the life I wanted so I looked for a new life, which would begin when I found someone to tell. That's what I've been doing, looking for someone. Suddenly we're in water, side by side, talking about our lives.'

'See. I mean it was them. Those two. They asked for it. They wanted different lives. Each looking for someone. That's why we picked them, right?'

'Right, but they only wanted "lively".'

'And "ordinary".'

'Bull's wool, they wanted magic.'

'Ordinary magic, not magic magic.'

'And just meeting could've been magic enough.'

'In a forest.'

'Even a coffee shop.'

'At a party.'

'Ti ti ti, you agreed at the time.'

'We didn't have time to think.'

'Well you should've planned it all out properly beforehand then. I mean all this fine twitter about helping fate. Think what happened to Maui when he tried that.'

'That? That was all your fault.'

'You and that silly giggle of yours.'

'Well I always get the blame for it, but can't you see it was a cracked idea in the first place? I saved the day is how I look at it.'

'That's because you've got big ideas about yourself.'

'Fact is we set off without a plan and had to think what to do when we got there.'

'And when we got there you just zapped your fan and the two of them were up to their armpits.'

'So happy and in love.'

'Full of false hope, full of jewellery, springs and things.'

'Ti ti ti, ti ti ti, it was great, wasn't it? Yous thought it was great. Go on, admit it.'

'That was then.'

'Now we got to do something.'

'Got to have a proper plan.'

'And that plan doesn't include you, Piwaka.'

'No, you're not coming.'

We talked and talked, about everything, every stitch of our lives — about moving from place to place, or about staying in one place, about searching, hoping, waiting, and knowing there could be a different life. Days and nights could have passed as we talked, and after a while our lives converged and we became part of each other's story.

And at the end of talking we made love as though there'd be no end to whirring, ticking, hammering, striking, springs, jewels and rainbows. Lively. Days and weeks could have passed for all we knew, or months and years.

At last it brought us ashore, and from there we set out together with no need to tell our separate stories. But did we take a wrong turn when we left the grey sea and shore which we had filled with falling, spinning light and colour?

That's how it seemed, because one day we found ourselves clinging together in greyness, trembling, all colour gone.

And after some time, after years perhaps, this greyness broke itself in two and everything, everywhere became separate.

So from then on we walked a chequered floor where we could walk in any direction as long as we walked together, as long as we were twinned, crosswired, or back to back with arms hooked through each other's in a push-me-pull-you game. White and black. Flicker flash.

But how can two people, destined to twin step forever, expect never to put one foot wrong, never to get out of step, never to end up on different squares whether side by side, back to back or facing each other? How can they, in the end, not find themselves once again, in different stories?

'Please yourselves. But I didn't mess up as much as you think.'

'Looks bad enough from this perch.'

'And this.'

'Well anyway, what's your big plan Miro and Toitoi?'

'What we'll do is we'll go and sit on their shoulders.'

'Kss ss ss ss. Is that it?'

'What's wrong with that?'

'What good'll that do?'

'Well you never know. I mean we deserted them, started something and left them to it. Now if we can get in close maybe?'

'Still I reckon we gave them enough liveliness to last for the rest of their days.'

'Well maybe we let them make a wrong turn.'

'Let them? I mean they did it. It was up to them.'

'So you'd just leave them then?'

'You don't care?'

'I didn't say that. Everyone always gets me wrong.'

'We're off, Piwaka.'

'I'm not as bad as yous all think.'

'Says you.'

Here I am. There's Maneta. Me on this black square and there's no light. She sits on white with her eyes closed, hunched forward and I can't see her heart. Or she has no eyes, has no heart.

Am I responsible for that?

When did it happen?

Should I call?

Should I call her name?

If I call will she be there?

Will she hear?

Maneta.

There's a touch on my shoulder but it's not Maneta. It's a touch of picky claws. It's lively. Could it touch my heart?

'Maneta.'

Is this my tombstone, this white square? But I don't want thoughts like that at all. I want my life.

There's Kata. I sense him in the dark. Whether his eyes are open or closed, whether he sits straight or hunched forward I don't know. But I know there's something missing from him that I think I stole. I can't remember what it is.

I could ask him.

I could call his name.

Kata.

There's a fluttering by my ear, a little tweaking of my lobe. Who's there? Should I call?

'Kata.'

'Did you hear that?'

'He called.'

'She called.'

'Kata.'

'Maneta.'

'Trouble is neither of them heard.'

'We'll just have to be patient.'

'Why don't we flap about, make a bit of a stir.'

'Mm, but I wonder how long for. I'm starving.'

'Me too.'

'I mean it was a long way.'

'I'm tired.'

'Me too.'

'Now we're stuck here, if we give up now it'll be just like last time.'

'Even worse, because nothing's happening. They can't even hear each other.'

'I was homesick actually, last time, all that water.'

'Sick for trees.'

'I'm homesick again.'

'Me too.'

'I'm starving.'

'Me too.'

'These two, all they do is mope.'

'Let out a bleat now and then.'

'How're we going to get through to them?'

'Sss sss sss, through their ears, dummies.'

'You?'

'Get lost you.'

'We don't want you here messing things up.'

'I brought you some food.'

'Well . . .'

'Thanks.'

'What do you mean, through their ears?'

'You mean talk to them?'

'Course. Shout. Remind them how their eyes shone, ticked, whirred. Let them remember their gold, their pull-starts, their cock and jenny, their springs, their spangles and jangles. Tell them about their screws, dumbells.'

'You reckon?'

'Course.'

'We could try.'

'But no giggling.'

'Okay.'

There's something around. I feel it. And I remember something that happened, long ago. It was to do with my life. It was to do with Maneta.

'You're getting it, you're getting it. Keep trying. Ropy sea, remember. Ticking eyes.'

I looked at her, she looked at me. I wondered what we were doing there but I didn't care. I was full of joy and love. Who said that? We made love, we talked about our lives.

'You got it, you got it.'

'Kss ss ss, ti ti ti ti.'

'Shut up you.'

Which should have been enough to last, but we thought we

could go together all the way, we thought we could be each other. The road we found together was not always wide enough for two.

'And how do you feel about us being in your story?'

'Kss ss ss, what's that got to do with it, you're losing it, Toitoi.'

'Sorry.'

I think I hear my name.

Something's biting my ear and I haven't the energy to find out what it is. I called Kata but he didn't answer me, or didn't hear.

But anyway I suddenly thought of something that happened a long time ago. There was gold light sluicing up grey water into coloured bands. Kata was yelling at the top of his voice, to the clouds, to the sky. It was marvellous.

'Keep it up, keep it up. What about dangle and spangle?'

'Ti ti ti ti, ss ss ss.'

'Shove off before you spoil everything.'

'Tell her, tell her. There was enough to last them all their lives.'

'This is fun, talking in her story.'

'Concentrate, can't you, Miro?'

We should've left our hands free, abandoned old luggage, because there was no room for it on the road we took. But there must be different roads we can try, that we can meet along from time to time and find joy. Is that Kata calling?

'He heard.'

'She heard.'

'They're standing.'

'Walking towards each other.'

'That's good.'

'That's good.'

'That's it.'

'That's it, then. We did it.'

'They'll find out where they missed the turn.'

'Chuck out all the old stuff. Start again.'

'I mean we did it, didn't we?'

'Ti ti ti, it's pretty ordinary magic if you ask me.'

'Who asked?'

'We can go home now.'

'Kss ss ss, I don't think so.'

'What do you mean?'

'I reckon you're stuck here for good, that is if you want to see this thing through. If you start something you've got to finish it, remember. Otherwise your nest falls out of the tree.'

'Tree?'

'I'd give anything for a tree.'

'It's not fair.'

'You got us into this, Piwaka.'

'Now you better get us out of it.'

'Wimps ... Well, tell you what then, we'll give them a bit of magic magic, enough to last a while, say ten years. Then yous can get off home for ten years.'

'I suppose.'

'If that's the best you've got to offer, but tell us what you're going to do first.'

'Okay, let's see. They could be riding on clouds, bird clouds, feathered red and orange ...'

'We were thinking of forests, actually ...'

'They'll be dressed in leather and silver and holding flaming torches, ribbons on their heels riding across the skies ...'

'Romantic twit ...'

'Side by side ...'

'No, no, you didn't listen, not too much side by side. They want some different roads.'

'They don't want to be glued, just to live in the same story.'

'So they reckon, but I . . .'

'No buts.'

'But if . . .'

'No ifs.'

'Okay, Okay. Riding across the skies anyway they want to go, apart or together . . .'

'That's better.'

'Under emerald stars. And there's music — guitars and violins, flutes and cymbals, animal dancers, flares and a rain of flowers.'

'Hey, taihoa.'

'Yeah, taihoa. Overkill, if you ask us.'

'Huh, I can always go home if yous don't like it.'

'No, no, it's okay, just kidding, as long as it means we can leave them for a while.'

'Crimson clouds to roll in when they fall together.'

'Yeah, yeah, let's do it then.'

'Yes come on, Piwaka, give them a flick.'

'Then we can tail on out.'

'Home.'

'To trees.'

'For the next ten years.'

'Sweet, sweet trees.'

'And we can watch from there.'

The Women's Press is Britain's leading women's publishing house. Established in 1978, we publish high-quality fiction and non-fiction from outstanding women writers worldwide. Our exciting and diverse list includes literary fiction, detective novels, biography and autobiography, health, women's studies, handbooks, literary criticism, psychology and self help, the arts, our popular Livewire Books for Teenagers young adult series and the bestselling annual *Women Artists Diary* featuring beautiful colour and black-and-white illustrations from the best in contemporary women's art.

If you would like more information about our books, please send an A5 sae for our latest catalogue and complete list to:

The Sales Department
The Women's Press Ltd
34 Great Sutton Street
London EC1V 0DX
Tel: 0171 251 3007
Fax: 0171 608 1938

Also of interest:

Patricia Grace
Cousins

Award-winning novelist, Patricia Grace, paints a resonant portrait of three very different women connected by a common background, thrown together as children and now grown apart as adults.

Mata is always waiting — for life to happen as it passes her by. Missy is the observer — accepting things as they are but nurturing her dreams. Maraketa is the chosen one — carrying her family's hopes with her. Despite their differences, the three cousins are united in adversity, brought together by the strength of their shared culture and spiritual traditions.

'Very moving...More than a powerful saga of the experience of Maori women. It is an exploration of love and the need to belong.'
Mary Scott, *Everywoman*, Top Ten Novels of the Year

'Lucid and skilful...Vivid and truthful.' *The Observer*

Fiction £5.99
ISBN 0 7043 4355 X

Patricia Grace
Potiki

From one of New Zealand's finest writers comes a beautifully
told story of a small Maori coastal community whose land and
way of life are threatened by developers. At the centre of the
conflict are Granny McDonald, the community's consistent
source of calm and reason, and Tokowaru-i-te-Marama, the
prophet child, who can see with sinister accuracy the advent of a
new and horrifying era. Together, they sustain a vision in which
the community can survive against all odds...

**'Real and compelling...This novel transcends time and
place.'** *Los Angeles Times*

Fiction £3.95
ISBN 0 7043 4081 X

Livewire Books for Teenagers

Patricia Grace
Mutuwhenua
The Moon Sleeps

Nineteen-year-old Ripeka and her large Maori family live in quiet
and seemingly forgotten rural New Zealand. Restless and bored,
Ripeka longs for excitement, changes her name to Linda, and falls
in love with Graeme, a Pakeha school teacher.

Though her family are frightened for her and disapprove, the
couple marry and move away. But Linda can't adjust to the
strange ways of the city. Missing the spiritual life and support of
her own people, she is soon forced to make some harsh
decisions for the future...

Renowned author, Patricia Grace, paints an absorbing picture of
conflicting values between cultures, old and new, young and old,
in this intense and exciting novel for young adults.

Fiction £2.95
ISBN 0 7043 4911 6

Marion McLeod and Lydia Wevers, editors
One Whale, Singing
Stories from New Zealand

Showcasing the very best in women's writing, *One Whale, Singing*
brings together a compelling collection of stories from Janet
Frame, Keri Hulme, Patricia Grace, Rosie Scott and many more.
From Frame's mesmeric portraits of daily rural life to Keri
Hulme's tales of urban conflict, this superb anthology offers an
absorbing view of the world from original and intriguing new
vantage points.

'A celebration of excellence.' *Tribune*

**'An exciting collection...partly familiar, partly foreign,
wholly fascinating.'** *The Times*

Fiction £4.95
ISBN 0 7043 4014 3

Helen Windrath, editor
The Women's Press Book of New Myth and Magic

'But some folks say no, it's not that mountain sitting back watching over us, and it's not that black lake reaching, and it's not that old white-trunked, yellow-tipped tree next to Blue's that Reverend Daniles swears covers a hole leading from this world to the next. The thing that makes Pearl a funny kind of place is all that whispering we hear coming up from the ground.'

In this entrancing, powerful and acclaimed collection, women explore alternatives to the highly prized values of finance, commercialism and practicality, illustrating their relationship to mythology and magic, both in terms of women's great inner strengths, and in their interaction with the outside world.

'**A delicious, delirious brew . . . a lot of fun.**' *Everywoman*

'**You will be hooked . . .**' *The Voice*

Fiction £7.99
ISBN 0 7043 4347 9

Velma Wallis
Two Old Women
An Alaska Legend of Betrayal, Courage
and Survival

Two old women are abandoned by their migrating tribe as it faces
starvation brought on by an unusually harsh winter. Forsaken for
their weaknesses, the two women show a surprising resilience
and strength, forging their own journey and eventually averting
tragedy for the whole community...

Few books have generated such excitement and enchantment as
Velma Wallis' powerful retelling of this ancient Alaskan legend –
passed down from mother to daughter over generations. An
instantaneous and universal success, it has been translated into
twelve languages worldwide, taking readers and critics by storm.

**'Beautiful and moving...Her writing is as lean and
muscular, as full of unexpected bounties, as the far
north.'** *Washington Post*

'My favourite book since *The Color Purple*.'
Feminist Bookstore News

**'When you've read this book, you will feel that you are a
slightly better person than you knew you were.'**
Ursula K Le Guin

Fiction £5.99
ISBN 0 7043 4424 6